Getting Ready
to
Preach

Getting Ready to Preach

Robert H. Spain

ABINGDON PRESS/Nashville

GETTING READY TO PREACH

Copyright © 1995 by Abingdon Press

This book is printed on recycled, acid-free paper.

Library of Congress Cataloging-in-Publication Data

Spain, Robert H., 1925–
    Getting ready to preach/Robert H. Spain.
        p.   cm.
    Includes bibliographical references.
    ISBN 0-687-00616-3 (pbk.: alk. paper)
    1. Preaching.   2. Clergy—Office.   I. Title.
BV4211.2.S66   1996
251'.01—dc20   95-39957
                                                              CIP

Scripture quotations, unless otherwise indicated, are from the New Revised Standard Version Bible, copyright © 1989, by the Division of Christian Education of the National Council of the Churches of Christ in the United States of America.

Scripture quotations noted KJV are from the King James Version of the Bible.

95 96 97 98 99 00 01 02 03 04—10 9 8 7 6 5 4 3 2 1

MANUFACTURED IN THE UNITED STATES OF AMERICA

C O N T E N T S

CONTENTS

P R E F A C E

One of the greatest privileges given to a pastor is the opportunity to "preach the Word." There is no way to overstate the spiritual experience of being allowed to share God's word with a congregation. Most of us would rate this part of our work at or near the top of everything we do.

Several years ago certain groups declared that preaching had been "oversold," and really wasn't the big event many believed it to be. "Our time," they said, "should be spent in other things." However, another group never believed those words. They were the people who sat in the pews of our churches. Our congregations rate "preaching" as very important.

It is true that they want us to be good pastors, good counselors, good administrators, good fund-raisers and good community-relations persons, but in their letters and visits to my office as a bishop, they spoke more about wanting a "preacher" than anything else.

In the Bible, our work is often described as being a herald of the King, for they were the ones who delivered the word of the King to others. The word did not originate with them. They were the messengers. They ran with the news. This image became even more meaningful when Jesus gave the disciples (and us) the commission to go into all the world and proclaim [preach] the Word.

As the church validates our call to ministry, we remember the words from *The United Methodist Book of Worship*, "Take the authority to preach the Word . . ." Preaching is not our total responsibility, but it is important—very important.

PREFACE

I write to you as a practitioner, and as a fellow traveler in the ministry who takes seriously the call of God upon my life. Like you, I take the commission to preach seriously. I do not face the subject of preaching as one with all the answers. I have spent my life in the Lord's field, and I write to you as one still learning and still hoping to find a way to proclaim the Word better.

A sign in an English antique shop announced: "Nothing New Here." That tells the story. I have very little to share that is unique or secretive. I haven't discovered a secret door that opens automatically to "good preaching." I know of no easy road. If it were not for the joy and excitement of preaching, I would use the words of Winston Churchill when he said, "I have nothing to offer but blood, toil, tears and sweat." Preaching is exciting, but it's also tough work.

Some of Jesus' last words were that we would never be left to our work alone. "I will be with you." When I read or hear these words I want to offer the response so often used in our prayer liturgies, "Thanks be to God." Preaching is not a one-person endeavor. The preparation (and delivery) of a sermon is always a partnership between the pastor and God. We are the heralds, and as such we are the ones physically seen, but the Holy Spirit is our faithful guide. At times pastors make the boastful claim that it is all up to the Lord. We must never leave God out of it, but neither can we excuse ourselves. We are in it. Facing a congregation week after week with a fresh and meaningful message requires a prayer life and scripture study beyond anything most people can imagine. Learning to cope with such a heavy, although rewarding and exciting, responsibility is a lifelong quest for a pastor.

Since God is everywhere, we can count on his working alongside us as we prepare to preach, which means allotting more time than the week before the sermon is to be preached to sermon preparation.

PREFACE

The focus of this book is on God's call to us, the need for faithfulness, and the preparation for preaching. This preparation begins with examples of tools relating to the accumulating and storing of ideas and thoughts. Next are suggested blueprints, crafting possibilities, and evaluations of effective preaching followed by a brief look at the preparation of the preacher.

You have been chosen! What a responsibility! What a privilege!

Called to Be a Worker

Chosen!

Preaching begins with an initiative from God. Seeing the hurt of the world and hearing the cries, God sent his Son to prepare the way so that all could have a new and meaningful life. Through the life, death, and resurrection of Jesus, the way to God was opened for all. The veil separating the world from God was torn asunder. Through Jesus Christ, life could be filled with meaning and purpose.

To herald this good news, God called you—and me. In John 15:16 the call is explained. "You did not choose me but I chose you. And appointed you to go and bear fruit, fruit that will last."

The apostle Paul spoke about it: "Called to be an apostle, set apart for the gospel of God" (Romans 1:1). Later he declared to the church at Corinth: "An obligation is laid on me, and woe to me if I do not proclaim the gospel!" (I Cor. 9:16). The KJV says, "necessity is laid upon me." A call is a must.

In most people's minds, a "call" from God is a fuzzy notion. We know that God has invited us to salvation in Christ, which indeed is a calling. We know that God has invited and called all baptized Christians to be a part of the Kingdom's work. We know as pastors that the work of lay persons in the church is as important as anything we may do, so how do we explain our special call to ministry?

Louis Armstrong, the famous trumpeter, was once reportedly asked to define "jazz." He thought for a moment and said, "If you gotta ask you'll never know."

Almost the same thing can be said about our call to the ministry. If you need to ask, no definition will do any good.

In most schools guidance counselors help students uncover possible career and vocational choices. Using a battery of tests, a wise counselor directs students toward areas of work that appear best suited for them.

Ministry is different. It is not an option from a skills-assessment program. As the apostle Paul said, this work is "laid" upon us. We do not choose it. There is a world of difference between choosing the work of ministry and being chosen for it.

A few years ago, Dr. Pierce Harris was a well-known preacher in Atlanta. His reputation as a colorful character was almost as well known as his preaching. Stories about him are plentiful and often repeated.

One night after an evening worship service, a young man came up to him and said, "Dr. Harris I am thinking about taking up the profession of the ministry, and I would like to talk with you about it."

Dr. Harris was never known as a conversationalist and said, "Well son, there is no need for us to talk. I can tell you right now. Don't do it!" There was a startled look on the young man's face, but Dr. Harris continued.

"It's a very, very poor profession. In the first place, they don't pay you very much for what they expect you to do. You have to study harder than a teacher and have more enthusiasm than an insurance salesman. You have to make more speeches than a lawyer, and more house calls than a doctor. Besides all that, you have to be the administrator of an adult nursery. Take my advice. Don't do it."

After a long pause, he added, "Don't go into it as a profession, but if in the stillness of some hour, a power comes over your soul, a feeling of the eternal working within you, and you hear God asking, 'Whom shall I send?' then don't let anything in the world dissuade you from answering, 'Here I am. Send me.' The ministry is a poor profession, but it's a tremendous calling."

The apostle Paul spoke for all of us when he said, "Everyone who calls on the name of the Lord shall be saved. But how are they to call on one in whom they have not believed? And how are they to believe in one of whom they have never heard? And how are they to hear without someone to proclaim him? And how are they to proclaim him unless they are sent?" (Romans 10:13-15).

Being chosen does not give one a special place, but a special responsibility. "If I proclaim the gospel, this gives me no ground for boasting" (I Cor. 9:16). There is nothing to boast about. Ministry is a "sent" work. It is "laid" upon us. We do not choose it. It chooses us.

Not the Same for Everyone

God does not call everyone in the same way. For the first twenty-three years of my life, I never for one moment had even a fleeting thought of being a minister. With my family I regularly attended Sunday school and worship. At our home, there were never any options about what we would do on Sunday. We were a church family, but it never crossed my mind that the ministry was a possibility for me.

After high school at the ripe age of 17 and World War II in progress, I joined the Navy with the condition that I would serve as a hospital corpsman. My career goal was to become a doctor. While in the Navy I became a laboratory technician and progressed well.

After the war I entered college as a premed student majoring in chemistry and minoring in bacteriology. I also worked at night in a hospital.

After completing my premed work, something unexpected happened. It's difficult to explain. There were no streaks of lightning, thunder, or special church services, yet I felt a sense of being led into a new field. For the first time, the idea emerged of serving God through the church.

I could not ignore the feeling of oughtness. I have doubted many things in my life, but I have never for one moment doubted that I was called into the ministry. Some of my colleagues struggled with their call for years, which for them became a long period of turmoil. For me, it was not that way. It was an immediate sense of letting God have my life.

God speaks to some people through the ability and graces that he has given them. He speaks to others through a concern and compassion for people that is beyond ordinary caring. Still others have been filled with a hurting concern for the future of the world. Sometimes God speaks through doors that seem to be opening or closing. And for a few, God's call takes a dramatic turn like the experience Paul had on the Damascus road.

The prophet Amos was a small town herdsman and a dresser of sycamore trees, but the Lord called him out, "and the LORD took me from following the flock, and the LORD said to me, 'Go, prophesy to my people Israel'" (Amos 7:15).

In the call that God gave to Jeremiah, he declares that he "called" him even before his birth. "Before I formed you in the womb I knew you, and before you were born I consecrated you; I appointed you a prophet to the nations" (Jer. 1:5). On many occasions God's Word came to Jeremiah. "Now the word of the LORD came to me saying" (Jer. 1:4).

CALLED TO BE A WORKER

Probably the most dramatic call that God gave to anyone came to Isaiah. His situation was far different from others. While mourning the passing of King Uzziah, he heard a cry from God for help. "Whom shall I send, and who will go for us?" (Isa. 6:8).

This cry was made even more powerful by the presence of seraphs that sang of the holiness of God. The house shook and was filled with smoke. Then a seraph with a live coal touched his lips blotting out all his sin. After all this, there could be no doubt in Isaiah's mind that God was at work in his life.

Today, the call of God is coming to many who are older than the typical new pastor. Most are second career people. We speak of this as a new phenomena, but it is not really new.

Many that God called in ancient times were also second career people. Moses was already working in another field when the Lord called him. And Matthew was a tax collector for Rome before Jesus touched his life and called him to be a follower.

Age or position has never been a problem for the Lord. Samuel was a young lad when he heard God's call. Abram was old. Many have been called from well-educated and socially prominent families, while others have come from humble surroundings and have few or no impressive academic credentials.

Currently, one of the most notable movements of God is the call of more women to the ministry. God has always called women but probably never as powerfully as today. In all parts of the world, women are providing dramatic Christian leadership.

The call of God is always a bit mysterious. Whenever I hear about the television series called *Unsolved Mysteries* I think about our call to the ministry. It is beyond our comprehension, and we should never take it for granted.

We all wonder about our call. Even Jeremiah questioned God about his call, "Ah, Lord GOD! Truly I do not know how to speak, for I am only a boy" (Jer. 1:6).

Just think about it: The God that put this whole world together, the God that worked for centuries to bring his people into a loving and right relationship with himself, the God that sent his own son into the world that his dream could be fulfilled—this same God put his hand upon you and me. I have never doubted it, but I have never understood it.

The Task

I have heard that in one of the newsrooms of a newspaper office hangs a huge banner which reads, "Bad news is good news. It's the news that keeps us in business."

Sadly, it is bad news that dominates much of what we hear and read, but we have been chosen to be the bearers of good news. Through Jesus Christ, good news has been sent into the world and it is our task to proclaim it in every way possible.

In the beginning of Jesus' ministry, he stood in the synagogue and read from the scroll of Isaiah. It said, "The Spirit of the Lord is upon me, because he has anointed me to bring good news to the poor. He has sent me to proclaim release to the captives and recovery of sight to the blind, to let the oppressed go free, to proclaim the year of the Lord's favor" (Luke 4:18-19). And then with the eyes of all those in the synagogue upon him, he said, "Today this scripture has been fulfilled in your hearing" (Luke 4:21).

Near the end of Jesus' life, while praying he said, "As you have sent me into the world, so I have sent them" (John 17:18). It is clear that the task given to Jesus was then given to his disciples and to us.

God's work has become our work. We are to offer hope to those who are discouraged and burdened. We are to help those who are struggling with life, to offer meaning and purpose to those who have lost their direction, and to provide light to those who are walking in darkness.

What a mother's arms are to a child who is frightened in the middle of the night, we are to those who are afraid and uncertain about life. What a life jacket is to those who cannot swim and have been thrust into the sea, we are to be to those who are in sin and are without help.

We are to expose the arrogance and pride of people, and teach and exemplify humility. We are to bring broken people into a close relationship with the one who can put the brokenness of their lives back together again. We are to announce a new day for all people. We are to offer redemption to those who are lost and welcome them back to the Father. We are to be the guides for those who are lost. We are to deliver good news to the world.

The work to which we have been called is spoken about throughout the Bible. Much of it can be summarized through four images—a herald, an ambassador, a shepherd, and a servant. All of them speak directly to our task, and no one of them can be neglected.

With the exception of several Advent hymns and scripture selections, the word *herald* is not a part of our everyday vocabulary. In the Bible the word was used for those who carried the news of the king. They did not just carry it, they ran to take it to the people. The herald was the bearer of the word.

Stories abound about the early days of riverboats on the Mississippi River, before radar and other sensory devices, about men whose task it was to constantly measure the depths of the river. They had their own vocabulary. They would cry out, "Mark four, mark trey, mark twain." In stormy and rough weather the captain, on the bridge of the ship, could not hear the marksmen as they called. So they used intermediaries who were called word-bearers. It was their job to listen intently and accurately pass on what they heard from those signaling the marking.

This speaks to our ministry. Halford Luccock was fond of saying that the minister is a channel and not the source. We do not initiate the word. We are to listen as carefully as we can and deliver it accurately to others. The apostle Paul spoke of this as giving a clear trumpet sound. If the sound is unclear and muffled, the people will not know what to do.

A few years ago, there was a period when preaching was declared unimportant. One group, the laity in our churches, never harbored such thoughts.

Our people may not often express it, but those who attend church each Sunday are hungry for some word from the Lord. They are crying and hungering for something that will sustain them through the days ahead. They want to know if God has something for them.

We must preach like we believe it will make a difference; and if we do, it will.

Occupying a pulpit on Sunday in front of a congregation is an awesome responsibility. There is no way to fully grasp it.

Once I officiated at the funeral of a member of the House of Representatives. Several planeloads of dignitaries from Washington arrived at the church resulting in almost a third of the entire House and Senate being present.

A colleague passed me on the way to the sanctuary and said, "You'd better be good today. You're preaching before the leaders of this country." His words didn't help my anxiety, but the fact is that we who preach Sunday after Sunday speak before the King of kings every time we enter the pulpit. Preaching is a powerful part of our ministry. We must do it well.

Robert Cueni in *The Vital Church Leader* says, "In your preaching, prepare every sermon as if it were to be delivered on Easter Sunday."

Others have suggested that we prepare and deliver every sermon as if it were the last one we would ever have the opportunity to preach.

Norman Shawchuck in *Leading the Congregation* reminds us that "any competent skyrocket can go off in a blaze of glory . . . once!" Our task, however, demands our best week after week. All facets of ministry are important, but nowhere is excellence more needed than in our preaching.

It's an Interesting Work

You have been called to represent God—to be his personal ambassador, and to share his message that salvation is for all who will receive it. Yet your work is subject to the approval of a congregation. You are called of God, set apart, but subject to the whims and desires of humans. I've always found this to be interesting. You may even have a stronger word than *interesting.*

You have been called to change people's lives, many of whom do not want to be changed. God expects you to take others from where they are to where they need to be, and some of them do not want to budge an inch. At the same time, you expect these same people to pay your salary.

You have been called to be responsible for programs of ministry and yet you have no real authority over anyone. You work primarily with volunteers who may or may not want to follow your leadership.

You have been called to proclaim the word every week and do it with power and might, yet your days may be totally consumed by demands which rob you of any prayer or preparation time.

You have been called to high and holy adventures that are absolutely essential to the kingdom of God, but your life is often so besieged with trivial brushfires that you have difficulty being about the things that God called you to do.

Are you sure ministry is what you want to do?

A construction crew was laying a drain line as part of a new building project. While excavating, the workmen uncovered a cable directly in their path.

The foreman called an electrician who was working nearby. The electrician looked at the cable and assured the foreman that the cable was dead. "Just cut it out of your way." "Are you sure there is no danger," the foreman asked. "Absolutely," was the reply. The foreman then asked, "Well . . . then will you cut it for us?" The electrician hesitated a moment, and with a slight smile said, "I'm not that sure!"

Are you sure ministry is what you want to do? Are you absolutely sure? These questions are important because I do not know of any work that is more demanding or filled with more stress.

Recently I have been reading about some of the early pioneer circuit riders who served the frontiers of this developing nation. Historians are fond of holding them up as ministers who served in the toughest of times. I do not want to take anything from them. They were a noble and courageous group. We are heirs of their faithfulness, but I doubt there has ever been a more demanding time for those in our calling than now. The only period which will require more time is the time immediately before us. Sure, I know, it is rewarding. It is great. It is fulfilling. It is all those good words, but it's tough.

The corporate world is changing so rapidly that it is difficult for even the main players to keep pace. There probably has never been a time with as many business mergers, buyouts, and failures as we are currently experiencing. Management systems are revised overnight and many who thought they were secure in their positions have been disillusioned.

The business world is changing, but no area is changing more rapidly than the church. The changing world has affected the church far more than many realize and ministering in and through the church has a new face. Ministry is tough now, but hold your hats. You've seen nothing yet!

We Are Not in the Work Alone

Take heart! Preaching is not a one-person endeavor. Jesus said that we would never be left to work alone. He promised to be with us. When I hear these words, I want to offer the response so often used in prayer liturgies: "Thanks be to God."

The Scriptures are filled with examples of God working with his chosen people. When the Israelites were hungry, he provided the food. Did he not give Gideon what was needed to be victorious? The door to the promised land was opened when there seemed to be no way.

God did not call us into this work to leave us stranded in some remote desert. We can rest assured that God will work alongside us. We are not alone.

As I contemplated my future in medicine while still in college, I realized that my communication skills were poor. I was a very timid person, and had difficulty talking to people. I decided that if I was going to be a doctor, I needed help in that part of my life.

I talked with my school counselor who recommended that I take a course in public speaking. Although I had taken some difficult courses before and survived, this was the scariest thing I had ever undertaken.

It was a horrible experience. Those were the days of the Dick Tracy character "Mumbles" and that became my nickname in that class. I performed so poorly that the professor openly acknowledged (to my embarrassment) that he gave me a B for effort and not for accomplishment. He strongly recommended that I take the class again for another semester. I did, but it wasn't any better than the first time.

At the end of that second semester, our final exam was to give a two minute after-dinner speech at a banquet. I worked hard on it, but it was a colossal blunder. My professor realized my poor showing and came over to me (with all the class looking on) and said a few words to the class about my effort.

He then said something I will never forget: "Spain, I am glad to have had you in my class. You have made a valiant effort to learn to speak in public. I have one word of advice for you and that is for you to never try to make your living with your voice."

I envy people who have those magnificent voices and can speak with power and eloquence. I envy those persons who have radiant personalities and can motivate congregations with their presence. I am not one of them, but I am one that God has called; and because he did call me, he has given me enough to serve him. I wish I had more, but whatever I have is a gift from God.

When God calls, he gives enough raw materials for us to cultivate and use. There is a part for God to play and a part for us as well. Most of us do not have everything we want, but when God calls us, he does not leave us alone.

Let's Get Moving!

Robert Fulghum's book, *All I Really Need to Know I Learned in Kindergarten,* tells of a French criminologist named Emile Locard who came up with an idea called "Locard's Exchange Principle," which states that any person passing through a room or life unknowingly deposits something there and also takes something away. Each of us is leaving something here and each of us is taking something away. What role do you want to play in the world during the next ten to twenty years? What difference do you want to make?

God called you to go and bear fruit, the kind of fruit that endures. He is not interested in short-range survival things. He wants the children of the world to be one family. Jesus opened the door for this to happen, and you are here to proclaim the good news.

Ministry is not something one decides to do. Ministry is a positive response to God's call. The initiative came from God. The response came from you. I'm proud God called me. I'm proud to be a minister. In the eyes of the world, the ministry may be a poor profession, but it's a great calling. Let's get to work.

CHAPTER TWO

Roadblocks to
Faithfulness

In the middle sixties, I was wandering over Israel traveling some of the same roads and visiting some of the places Jesus visited. One day I traveled from Jerusalem to Emmaus. En route I discovered the road was blocked by huge tank traps that had been placed there during the six-day war. Imagine roadblocks on the road to Emmaus, the road Jesus traveled.

Unfortunately, there are roadblocks along all spiritual roads. As clergy, we often define and describe for our congregations these "blocks" to spiritual maturity. We wax eloquently and warn our people to stay clear of them.

What we often forget is that there are blocks on the roads we travel also. Every profession or vocation is lined with roadblocks that keep a person from doing what he or she wants to do, or from being the person he or she wants to be. It is no different for those called into ministry. God's call does not guarantee uninterrupted travel.

There are at least ten possible roadblocks to effectiveness as a preacher. Although each preacher may not struggle with all of them, many confront one or more over the course of their ministry.

1) Isolation. In hospitals, isolation wards keep patients with communicable diseases away from others. Sometimes we build isolation areas for ourselves. People often talk about the isolation of college professors who live behind their cloistered ivy-covered walls, and many people also refer to clergy in much the same way.

A friend who is absolutely sure that we who are clergy do not know anything about the "real world" has often said, "I wish you people would come out of your holy places occasionally and see what goes on in the real world." He thinks we are shielded from the habits and trials of the world.

I don't agree with my friend, but there is the possibility of becoming isolated from those to whom we should minister. In Jesus' day, even the religious leaders wouldn't venture near lepers, but Jesus did.

We talk much about the poor, the disenfranchised, and the homeless, but often we do not know a single one of them by name. We don't walk where they walk. We may drive by them or know where they hang out, but we keep our distance.

Jesus called us to heal the hurting and to bring deliverance to those who are without. We have to be with them to do it.

2) Callousness. Near my home, rock masons have been building a huge wall for months. They handle rough stones day after day. One day I asked, "How do you handle the blisters that get on your hands?"

"Oh," he said, holding up his hands, "these callouses protect me."

Nature's form of protection, a callous is made of layers of dead skin that create a barrier for the more sensitive skin underneath. Most of us as clergy do not have calloused hands, but we can develop spiritual callouses that protect us from feeling too deeply and getting hurt.

Sickness, pain, trouble, and death are constant companions to clergy, and as a result we have to get used to them. However, some of us become hardened in the process.

We have to keep our emotions under control because they are on a roller coaster of constant turmoil. We face a grieving family at 4:00 in the afternoon and hurry to perform a marriage ceremony that same evening. We visit the wheelchair brigade at the nursing home one minute and rush out to be at the children's Bible lesson the next.

It is sad when clergy develop protective coatings around their spirits. Feelings and hurt are a part of our calling. We should never allow tenderness and caring to atrophy and become spiritual callouses.

3) Popularity. The desire to be popular is a noble desire that turns into a horrible disease whenever it gets out of control. It is all right to want to be liked, loved, and accepted. We want to be a part of the crowd and be friends with everyone. The success of our work depends on the relationships we have with others.

When relationships are not good, that problem becomes another roadblock that is difficult to break through. Being unloved and unaccepted is a real barrier to ministry.

The roadblock to faithfulness comes when the desire to be popular is our focus, our motivation. Ministers walk a constant tightrope. God has sent us on a mission and given us a message to proclaim, but that message is not always what others want to hear.

We must bring comfort, but at the same time everything we preach about is not comforting. We cannot let our desire to be popular distract us from our more difficult prophetic work.

4) Procrastination. This is the thief that robs us of one of our most precious possessions—time. Most of us know what we should be doing, but getting around to it is often difficult.

We have all seen those round, silver-dollar-sized pieces of wood imprinted with the letters "T U I T." Usually given to each other in jest, almost everyone needs "a round tuit." It is difficult to get around to "it," whatever that "it" is for each of us.

In some businesses, such as factory assembly lines and overnight mail delivery services, procrastination is not tolerated. Quarterbacks who procrastinate are sacked. For us, it is different. We can get by procrastinating at least for a while.

Unlike many people, ministers do not punch time clocks, meet quotas, or have someone monitoring everything we do. Within limits, we make our own schedules, set our own agendas and go about our work without direct interference.

We probably would not want it any other way, but this freedom makes us especially susceptible to the temptation to procrastinate. We might do well to remember the words from Philippians 3:13: "This one thing I do." If these words are not clear enough, listen to James: "Anyone, then, who knows the right thing to do and fails to do it, commits sin" (James 4:17).

5) **Busyness.** There is a big difference between being busy and busyness. Working hard and staying committed to work are noble qualities for the minister. On the other hand, busyness is feverish activity that produces few results. It's like the beginning swimmer who thrashes around in the pool thinking that all that activity will keep him afloat.

Being busy is a worthy quality. We know that if we want something done, find a busy person to do it. The Lord also knew the value of the busy person, for he chose them regularly. David was busy looking for the sheep. Peter was busy casting the net. Matthew was busy collecting taxes. Even Saul was busy—busy persecuting Christians and their friends.

In most ordination services, ministers are urged to stay with the work and faithfully fulfill the responsibilities of ministry. If we do this, we will indeed be busy persons.

No clergy can ever do all that needs to be done. Having something to do is not the problem. The roadblock is losing the ability to focus on what's important, to know what one ought to do.

Many clergy think they are busy when they are only restless. They jump from one thing to another—run here and then there, but the purpose is unclear. Most of us who are football fans have seen someone with the ball running like mad from sideline to sideline but never advancing the ball. Sometimes we can identify with those players.

The following phrase from the Scriptures sums up busyness well: "While your servant was busy here and there . . ." (I Kings 20:40). When our activity, although good, is just here and there, without reason or purpose, we have run into the roadblock of busyness.

6) Dryness. Casey Stengel, the former baseball manager, said, "There are two kinds of baseball managers: managers who have been fired, and managers that will be fired."

Well, there are also two kinds of preachers: those who have lost their passion for the Lord and those who will. We all suffer some periods of spiritual dryness.

When anyone loses his or her enthusiasm about work, it is unfortunate, but when a minister's passion for Christ begins to wane, it is nothing short of tragic.

We preach to others about their spiritual dry times, reminding them about the need for constant renewal. What we often forget is that spiritual dryness can happen to us also.

It usually isn't the result of external factors. Rather, it happens because we settle down into the routines of our work. We neglect the mountains of transfiguration. We keep the doors closed to the prayer closet. We abandon the vision for ministry that God gave us. Our negligence is not deliberate. We unconsciously drift into it.

7) Compromise. Jesus faced this roadblock to faithfulness to his calling when he was taken into the wilderness to be tempted by the devil. The temptation was to compromise his calling. Satan urged Jesus to use his powers in a different way than intended by showing him a quicker way to accomplish things.

Likewise, the world is constantly offering us things if we will compromise our positions. The constant temptation is to water down the gospel. Do this, and the pews will be full. Do that, and people will flock to you. Do something else, and your popularity rating will soar.

The work Jesus gave us to do must never be compromised, still the minister faces that temptation every day.

8) Attitude. There is little more important for a preacher than a good attitude. The lack of it may be one of the largest stumbling blocks. How it is that one called of God should ever be detoured in this way is a good question, but again and again I have seen poor attitudes block the road to meaningful ministry.

The Carnegie Institute analyzed the records of ten thousand persons that were identified as "successful." From their research, they concluded that 15 percent of success was due to technical training and basic educational skills. The other 85 percent was due to personality, and the primary personality trait was attitude.

Similarly, William James said the greatest discovery of his generation was that our lives can be altered by our attitudes. Attitude is a condition of the mind and a mirror reflection of the inner self. Our attitude reveals our thoughts and feelings.

Through magnetic resonance imaging, technicians can, via pictures, show a cross section of the body at various angles. As yet, there is no machine that can reveal the spirit of a person, but this spirit is revealed by one's attitude. Romans 12:2 reminds us to ". . . be transformed by the renewing of your minds." A poor attitude will rob anyone of the possibility of a faithful ministry.

9) Holy of Holies. The Holy of holies was the restricted place in the temple reserved for the high priest on certain holy days. At the crucifixion, the veil separating this place from all others was destroyed.

Yet in a different way, many of us have fashioned our own Holy of holies, and we have depended on them to keep us near the Lord.

I am talking about our familiarity with holy things in general that we who are clergy touch and live near every day.

Holy things include the Bible, the Book of Worship, and our Prayer Book. We sing from the hymnal every week, often wear the cross, stand in pulpits dedicated to the Lord, clothe ourselves in regal, holy garments, spend much of our days in consecrated places and are generally regarded as representatives of the Lord.

All this is a part of our calling and work. The only problem comes when we begin to believe that these things and places provide a protective coating that isolates us from the world.

In the Middle Ages, monasteries provided a retreat from the outside. Many pastors have created their own little monasteries within their churches today. In Jesus' time, the Pharisees put too much value on rules, rituals, and holy things. We don't want to run up against this. Holy things are not protective fetishes. Religious garments do not guarantee a religious nature. The wearing of a cross does not keep one from sin. Standing at the altar with a chalice in our hands does not automatically fill us with righteousness or preserve our souls.

10) Sin. Sin is as much a roadblock to faithfulness for the clergy as it is for everyone else. In God's call to us, we were not vaccinated against it, so unfortunately, we are not immune. Sin is a constant, nearby companion for everyone. Martin Luther was so beset by his sinful nature that he often went to confession every hour.

In recent years, some people have revealed the sin prevalent among clergy, but most of us still live decent moral lives. We do not usually engage in that which would bring dishonor and disrepute to Christ, the church, or our families.

Nels Ferre, one of my professors in seminary, used to remind us, however, that sin is a condition of the self. It is a matter of being before it is a matter of doing. Usually, we can keep our acts under control, but the spiritual cleanliness of the inner being is another thing.

Most of us can identify with William Temple, the late Archbishop of Canterbury, who, as a student at Oxford, went to hear a famous American evangelist. The preacher impressed upon his student congregation the forgiveness of God quoting the text, "Though your sins be as scarlet, they shall be as white as snow" (Isa. 1:18 KJV).

Temple said, "Though I went to the meeting in a serious, inquiring spirit, I found myself quite unmoved, for, alas, my sins were not scarlet; they were gray, all gray. They were not dramatic acts of rebellion—but colorless, tired sins of omission, inertia, and timidity."[1]

From Michelangelo's famous story about chipping away the marble and setting free the angel within, many versions of the same idea have emerged. One of them had to do with the man who had a huge stone elephant in his front yard. When asked how he could have ever carved such a likeness, he replied that it was simple. He simply chipped away everything that didn't look like an elephant.

To be the person God wants us to be, there must be a constant chipping away of those things that hinder us. It could be envy or pride or excessive ambition, anger, impatience, pretentious piousness or many other such things. Only you will know what needs to be "chipped" away

31

from your life. Sin—big ones, little ones, moral ones, mental ones, known or unknown—will rob anyone of faithfulness.

These ten roadblocks will not line the street for all clergy, but they are often nearby waiting to be rolled into place if we are not careful and mindful of them. Some will discover other blocking stones. They come from everywhere and in all sizes. It is important that we be aware of them and try as best we can to make sure they do not block our journey.

Equipping Your Workshop

Finding the Workplace That's Right for You

In my spare time, I am a would-be woodworker. By "would be," I mean that I dabble a bit but spend most of my time dreaming and talking about working. Maybe you, too, have a project just waiting for the day you know is coming, the day you will "get with it."

At least I do have a good woodworking shop. I built it myself. I adapted a saltbox New England carriage house plan that included a cupola and a handsome weather vane.

Inside are 8 double cabinets, 24 feet of pegboard (dripping in hanging goodies ready to use), 30 feet of bench space, and 342 labeled drawers filled with interesting supplies.

This shop is equipped with a 30-year collection of machines, including a shaper, lathe, bench saw, joiner, air compressor, dust collection unit, and a fine collection of hand tools.

The placement of machines, cabinets, drawers, and benches evolved over many years of trial and error, and now everything is positioned for efficiency and production. Although it isn't perfect (nothing is), it is a suitable place to work.

Preachers need a workplace, too. My "preacher work-shop" contains a lifetime of accumulated experience. Pruning and rearranging is a regular need. For those of us in the itinerant ministry, we must recognize that work-places, like plants, occasionally need to be repotted and transplanted. The new ground may not be exactly like the previous space or what we hoped it would be, but if we make up our minds to adapt to new surroundings, we can usually make new spaces work.

As you know, church buildings are not always con-structed with the minister's workplace in mind, nor have ministerial residences always accommodated such places. The minister's workplace, seldom ideal, in the past ranged from the corner of a guest room to a cleaned-out area in a church basement.

Currently, however, many churches provide an office for the minister in the church building. This place is very important, because it is a space for counseling, meeting with church leaders and committees, answering mail, telephoning, devotional times, and writing reports and sermons.

Our needs differ. The apostle Paul reminded us that we are not all alike. God gives us different gifts, and we have different work styles. As a result, we don't approach our work of ministry in the same way, including our choice of places to work.

For some, the church office may be the ideal place to work; others may find themselves distracted by the de-mands of church management—unanswered phone calls, unfinished reports, and church calendars. Personal tem-perament usually determines whether we prefer the church office or a more secluded home office for duties such as sermon preparation.

If your preferred place to work on sermons is at home, you will have to take into consideration the size of your family and residence. The perfect home study may not be available, but if you are inventive, you can probably manage to partition off some space to call your own. What's important is that the space you choose allows for maximum production.

It is best to free yourself from distractions in your workspace. Get rid of clutter, and if you can't part with it, then at least hide it in a box with a lid. Slips of paper reminding you of "Things I Need to Do" and invoices waiting to be paid are not conducive to focusing on God.

If your current workspace is hindering rather than facilitating your ability to write sermons, then consider an alternative space. Once you have settled on the space and freed it of clutter, take an inventory of your "tool chest."

Take Advantage of Technology's Toys

Work Bench: With all the modern equipment available to assist you in your work, you will probably need a large, sturdy desk. A large table can work just as well. Choose a "work bench" that can hold the weight of heavy office equipment (even if you don't own any yet, it never hurts to be prepared) and one that will allow plenty of space to spread your work out.

Typewriter/Computer: Although most of us began our ministry with a typewriter, a computer with a printer are the most efficient timesaving tools developed thus far in our lifetimes. (Warning: Computers should be used like tools, not toys. No fair playing computer games when you should be working!)

Filing Cabinets: No office is complete without this essential storage space. File cabinets are available in various colors, styles, and materials. Regardless of your preference your filing cabinet is your resource center which holds a lifetime of work.

Telephone: Even though you may want to unplug it sometimes to prevent interruptions, no office is complete without one. Answering machines are relatively inexpensive and also handy for screening calls.

Copy Machine: Obtaining this piece of equipment may not be possible for everyone, but it is worth considering. There are some reasonably priced small versions that are designed for home use. Copy machines are helpful in the production of any type of work.

Fax Machine: Here is another example of the marvels of modern technology. Although hardly a necessity, the fax machine is an asset that allows you to send and receive messages much faster than by mail and without the sometimes unwanted interruption of a telephone call.

The Right Chair: This addition may seem frivolous to some, but choosing a good chair is more important than many pastors realize. I have two chairs, both chosen by and for me. One is used for my computer work, and the other for reading or study.

A kitchen or folding chair are inexpensive options, but other chairs designed specifically for office use, will prove to be more valuable additions to your workshop.

Miscellaneous Toys: There is no limit to the equipment available. You may want to purchase a cassette recorder and transcribing equipment. In addition to the larger items already mentioned, you will probably want to include the following on your shopping list: paper, pencils, pens, staplers, sticky notes, tape, and scissors—anything that you like to use when you work.

Assemble Indispensable Tools

Having covered the basics of equipment and furnishing for your workshop, now let's consider books, the minister's hand tools. We all have our favorites, but here are some possibilities to consider. Regardless of which ones you select, be sure to arrange them conveniently that they are literally at your fingertips:

Bibles: Three or four different versions in addition to your favorite one are an asset. Reading from several often increases our awareness and understanding of particular events.

Dictionaries: Biblical dictionaries are invaluable when working on sermons. An up-to-date unabridged English dictionary is also helpful. Many ministers find the dictionaries that are available on computer disks useful.

Commentaries: Although there is no way to keep all the commentaries on your desk, they should be placed as near to your workstation as possible. Over the years I have accumulated several bits and pieces of various sets of commentaries, but the two I have found especially helpful are *The Interpreter's Bible* and William Barclay's work on the New Testament.

Bible Atlas: This tool allows you to see the distances and terrain one encounters when traveling from Nazareth to Jerusalem or from Jericho to Cana. In order for us to speak in images, we have to have images in our minds. An atlas is a valuable tool even for those of us who have traveled and/or worked in Israel.

Hymnal: The hymnal is a resource for preaching. As the story of God's work in the world is told through stories, much is also told through the music of the ages. Hymnals are handy in coordinating the hymns chosen for worship with the sermon.

Book of Worship: Packed with helpful material, the Book of Worship is a constant source of insight.

In addition to the specified resources listed above, don't forget to gather all your favorite books into your workshop. Both religious and nonreligious books can provide material for illustrations. Reference books alone cannot supply all the information we need to write effective sermons.

I began this section with details about my woodworking shop. It is well equipped and functionally well arranged, but the workplace, tools, machinery, and filled drawers are only a means to an end. These items are used to craft new things. A well-fashioned shop is an aid for doing other things—but only an aid.

It is no different with a minister's study. It is good to have tools and equipment, but that's all they are, tools. Using them for the purpose of fulfilling your higher aim is what it is all about.

CHAPTER FOUR

Unlocking the Workshop

Make a Commitment

The worker must take responsibility for unlocking the workshop and gaining access to it before productive work can take place, regardless of how valuable the workshop or tools are. A worker committed to the task, who uses God as the source of inspiration, and the Holy Spirit as the catalyst, can accomplish great works.

According to several biographies and autobiographies, many of the great preachers devoted a significant amount of time to sermon preparation. Day after day, they retreated to their studies, their workplace, and searched the Scriptures. They pored over commentaries and wrote sermons.

Some devoted each morning, Monday through Thursday, to study, and all day Friday to writing. They spent Saturday allowing the sermon to fill them. No one questions how skilled these preachers were at their craft.

Ministry in current times is different. The responsibilities thrust upon the pastor have reached an explosive level. We as pastors may be partially responsible for all that is expected of us, but managing a church, counseling the hurting, organizing programs, running from committee to committee, balancing a budget, and visiting the sick leaves little time to spend in the sermon workplace. Occupying the workshop on a regular basis is difficult, but essential to writing good sermons.

An elderly friend, who is an attorney, and I were talking one day about all the courtroom drama television shows. The writers develop good plots and give the actors great lines. Then the actor lawyers show their skills at prosecuting and defending cases.

My friend said, "There is much to be appreciated about lawyers that have infectious personalities, a good use of words, charm, and persuasive powers. Those are all valuable in the practice of law, but most legal cases are not won in the courtroom before a jury. They are won in the attorney's study while preparing the case."

Notice the analogy between legal cases and sermons. Few clergy speak eloquently on any subject at any given time. Personality, charm, presence, and a facility with language are important in preaching, but most good sermons are not born in the pulpit. They come from sweat and toil in the study or workshop.

Making a commitment to devote adequate time to sermon preparation is essential. The difficulties encountered when trying to use time efficiently has plagued ministers of every age. John Wesley was so intent on faithfulness to his calling that every minute was crucial. He admonished us not to spend any more time on any task than was necessary. But pastors are not immune from the time-crunch felt by our society, which is characterized by "ready-to-wear" labels, timesaving devices, and quick-fix meals. Every project seems to come with a "rush" label on it.

To meet these demands, many of us have turned to time-management helps. Consultants are helpful, but time can't be managed by stretching, changing, or shrinking it. Time also can't be saved. It moves on. Ministry demands more commitment and efficiency than ever before.

In an attempt to sound complimentary, a layperson once said, "Our pastor goes to work every morning at 8:00 just like he had a real job."

Unlike most persons in the workplace who have supervisors to observe and monitor their progress, we are able to structure our own work schedule. We are accountable to our congregations and denominational groups, but we have a great deal of freedom in setting priorities and devising our methods of working.

Whatever difficulties may arise from either time constraints or a lack of understanding of our work, we must be faithful to our calling by being committed. Nothing happens until we make a commitment, whether we are talking about an exercise regimen, diet, or time to study. Thinking about it or dreaming about it is not the same as entering the workshop with determination.

Five Keys to Successful Work Habits

Ministry requires a rigid and demanding management of ourselves. Good work habits are essential. While every aspect of our calling demands attention and time, nowhere is it more important than in carving out uninterrupted time for study, prayer, and sermon preparation.

Our usefulness to the church and to the Lord depends upon it. The door to the study must be unlocked. Here are five keys.

Key Number One: Set Your Priorities Carefully

The Italian management consultant, Pareto, has established the principle that 20 percent of our time produces 80 percent of the results.

Determine what must be done today, this week, and this month. Priorities are signposts. It is not enough to be at work, we must also be working toward the highest and most important goals. If we don't know where we are going, we have little hope of meeting any objectives.

Brother Lawrence authored the medieval classic which many of us have studied, *The Practice of the Presence of God*. Brother Lawrence never hurried or worked quickly, yet he did twice as much as anyone else. His secret was to always work on things that needed to be done.

Viktor Frankl, the great Austrian psychiatrist, wrote, "Unless one wishes to drown, he has to become selective." We must become selective about everything we do, from the books we read, to the TV programs we watch, to deciding what to keep and what to throw away. We have to know what is valuable and what isn't, including the tasks before us.

Key Number Two: A Balanced Schedule

Strong scheduling skills are a must for clergy. Some pastors feel a calendar boxes them in, but the opposite is true. The less time you have available, the more important it is to keep a manageable schedule. If you don't schedule your time, someone else will.

Reserve time for personal study, and write it down on your calendar. This time must be as important as church board meetings, committee meetings, and counseling sessions. You have earned the right to designated time for spiritual reflection, study, and sermon preparation.

Billy Graham once said to a group of clergy in London that if he had his ministry to do over again, he would study three times as much and accept fewer preaching engagements.

Keep in mind your times of peak production as you arrange your schedule. Television network executives refer to this as "prime time." What time of the day do your creative juices flow? This time may differ for each of us. You may work best in the mornings. My best creative time is late at night.

Our body rhythms also tell us how many hours we can work productively at one stretch. Be sensitive to your body's signals so you can make the most of your time.

Equally important in the attempt to achieve a balanced life is to schedule personal family time. Consider your children's activities. Celebrate birthdays and take vacations. Do not be afraid to put these on your calendar. Remember, both the body and the mind need rest.

Karl Barth, in *Church Dogmatics*, wrote, "He who spends no time in rejoicing and who does not rest from his work despises God's goodness and faithfulness and puts his hope, not in God, but in his own work."

Scheduling ahead allows you to say no to certain people and events. This lesson is one of the most difficult for a pastor to learn because we want to be available all the time. We are pastoral, and we want to serve people.

There is nothing wrong with that attitude, but if we are honest there are more things than one person can reasonably do. It is nice to be wanted, but you cannot do everything. If you don't learn to say no, you will continually be in a state of shifting priorities.

Similarly, learning to say no helps us avoid becoming a workaholic. The workaholic labors under the illusion that success is measured by output; therefore one must be working all the time. It is helpful to remember one of Buddha's sayings: "Don't just do something; sit there."

In *While It Is Day* Elton Trueblood wrote, "A public person, though they are necessarily available at many times, must learn to hide. If he is always available, he is not worth enough when he is available."

I am reminded of the story about two men who had cut wood all day. One worked straight through without stopping to rest. At the end of the day, he had a sizable pile of logs. The other rested every fifty minutes. At the end of the day, his pile was taller.

"How could you chop more?" asked the first woodcutter. His friend answered, "When I stopped to rest, I also sharpened my ax."

Go to your study. Spend quality time with the Lord. Write sermons. Your people and God will be pleased.

Key Number Three: Work When You Work

This habit is difficult to cultivate. It is easy for clergy to think they are working when they are only thinking about it.

I heard a story of a man who was always getting ready to do something. In good Southern dialect, he was always "fixing to." He uttered this phrase so often that when he died, it was placed on his tombstone.

Much of our time is spent "fixing to" instead of working.

Learning to know the difference between work and play is imperative. Schedule time for both and don't blur the distinction between them.

Key Number Four: Practice the Fine Art of Delegation

In the church, we have built-in delegation in the form of church boards, trustees, councils and committees—each has a chairperson and an assigned agenda.

Delegation is a valuable management tool. It isn't really the right word for sharing our task of ministry because "delegation" implies that we are dispensing our own tasks to others. All baptized Christians are in ministry, and it is our task to recruit, equip, and turn them loose to minister.

In I Peter 4:10, we read, "Like good stewards of the manifold grace of God, serve one another with whatever gift each of you has received."

In Acts, we are told that the apostles couldn't do everything so they turned over some of the work to others: "And the twelve called together the whole community of the disciples and said, 'It is not right that we should neglect the word of God in order to wait on tables. Therefore, friends, select from among yourselves seven men of good standing . . . while we . . . devote ourselves to prayer and to serving the word'" (6:2). So we aren't the first to find ourselves in a time crunch.

Some lay people assume that the ministry belongs to the clergy. We need to turn this attitude around and cultivate lay people for real ministry—not just administrative duties.

Paul appointed, used, and depended upon elders as ministry partners in every church. He taught Titus to do the same. Every church should be pastored by a team rather than a single shepherd.

Consider these scripture passages: "After they had appointed elders for them in each church, with prayer and fasting they entrusted them to the Lord in whom they had come to believe" (Acts 14:23); and "I left you . . . that you should . . . appoint elders in every town, as I directed you" (Titus 1:5).

Delegation allows the workforce to grow and mature. It is easier for a teacher to write a sentence than it is to help children write one, but the job of the teacher is to help students perform for themselves. The teacher is the enabler. Their job is to help others develop their own skills and abilities so they can eventually function without the help of the teacher.

It is no different for the pastor of the church. Our task is to help people minister on their own. When the people with whom we work are full participants in both decisions and workload, their involvement increases their commitment and raises their morale. Delegation is not just a managerial procedure; it is a gift to people.

Delegation allows us to focus on those things that only the pastor can do.

Key Number Five: Handle Interruptions Efficiently

If you begin with a clear set of goals and have used the other four keys, you are on the right track. Unfortunately, we don't come equipped with the automatic-focus capabilities that some cameras have, so we must continually sharpen our own focus and not allow ourselves to become distracted.

One company uses the slogan, "Do It Now, Do It Now." It is plastered on every wall and desk. Some of us have inherited a gene that prompts this attitude, but some of us have not. It can be easy to put aside the report or delay the sermon until another time.

Set deadlines and remind yourself, "This work is mine. No one else will do it. It belongs to me." These reminders will enable you to handle interruptions more effectively than if you set no deadlines at all.

Of course, some interruptions are high-value tasks. Emergencies, such as death, accidents, or community mishaps are legitimate calls for ministry. You must respond to these.

However, a large number of interruptions rob us of valuable time and keep us from doing what we should. The four most common are drop-in visitors, brushfires, undue socializing, and the telephone.

We are trained to be pastoral, but some of us have never learned the difference between being pastoral and social. Being with people is part of our work, and having a cup of coffee or lunch with someone is not out of place for a pastor. However, we must be careful not to allow these activities to consume too much of our time.

People who drop in unexpectedly or who expect us to rush out and handle every request immediately need to learn that we are not available all of the time.

Similarly, the telephone, even though a marvelous tool, can consume too much time. Some pastors screen their calls. Others either do not have that privilege or do not want it. In these cases, it is doubly important to control how much time is spent on the telephone.

Acknowledge the Holy Spirit's Presence

We need to acknowledge the Holy Spirit's presence in our workshop. A few people may even go overboard and boast that "divine inspiration" is the wellspring for their words.

"Just open yourself up to the Spirit," they say. "God will give the message."

These words from Matthew are well known to them: ". . . do not worry about how you are to speak or what you are to say; for what you are to say will be given to you . . ." (Matt. 10:19). It is interesting that Jesus was not talking about preaching in that passage, but about appearing in a court of law. It was in that kind of situation, when adequate time for preparation would not be available, that the Spirit would guide the disciples in what to say.

John Stott, in *Between Two Worlds*, talks about a pastor who boasted all the time. The pastor said all the time he needed to prepare a Sunday sermon was the few minutes it took him to walk from the residence next door to the church.

The elders heard about his boastful claim and bought him a new residence—five miles from the church.[1]

Another man suffered a severe financial setback. His business failed and he became destitute. Finally in utter despair, he turned to God.

"Please God, you've got to help me. Help me win the lottery." But there was no answer to his prayer. The next day he prayed the same prayer, but again nothing happened.

This went on for days. The man thought that God was not listening. After a while, in desperation, he prayed, "I beg you, dear God, to help me win the lottery."

After a moment of silence, a voice came back to him saying, "Give me a break. At least buy a ticket."[2]

The work of the pastor is a partnership. We know the presence and power of God in the pulpit and in our studies. It is in the workshop that we "Give God a break" by making an investment.

Updating Your Toolbox

The Filing Cabinet

A sign in a cluttered, old-fashioned hardware store read, "We've got it if we can find it."

There is some truth to the saying, "If you want to lose something, put it in the filing cabinet." For some people, a filing cabinet is little more than an archive. However, it can become a viable resource center.

I am partial to my first filing cabinet. It was a gift from my wife on my first Christmas as a minister. Even though we've moved many times and added several additional filing cabinets, my first is a tool I prize. After 46 years, I still have the original key!

Many pastors choose to replace the old, gray-steel pull-drawer cabinets with their computer's amazing storage capacity. I cannot recommend this change. Computers are a tremendous addition to our work. I use one regularly, and do not know how I would work without one. But, for me, it has not emptied my other file cabinets. They still have value for me. I use both computers and cabinets, but for different purposes.

Store Nuts and Bolts of Illustrations

At the beginning of my ministry, I wanted to know how to store illustrations. I studied the methods others used and found most too complicated. Their systems were cumbersome and required too much cross-referencing.

Each of us has to discover a system that works best for us. However, since valuable information can be gained by exploring others' work, consider my system as you develop your own.

1) Never rely on your memory! Neurologists assure us that everything we read and hear is permanently stored in our brains. They tell us that nothing is ever lost, but they can't promise retrieval on demand. For that reason, no matter how time-consuming it is, write everything down—everything. This provides a backup copy on file even if both your memory and computer fail.

2) The four-by-six card. I mark illustrative material from everything I read or hear. Whenever I finish a book or magazine, I go back through it and put all the material I've marked on cards. If the illustration comes from a magazine, I usually tear it out and keep it in a file folder marked "Illustrations." Later the information is transferred onto index cards. If two or more cards are needed for one illustration, they are stapled together.

Hint: Some people prefer typing the illustrations directly into their computers. This is a matter of personal preference. The index cards work best for me.

3) Give each illustration a title. One word usually suffices and it is printed in capital letters, such as FORGIVENESS.

Following the one-word title, two or three descriptive words are added, such as FORGIVENESS—"conditions for," or "necessary for receiving." Beside the title CHURCH you might add—need to belong; or beside LEADERSHIP—necessary for visioning.

4) File everything alphabetically. Keep it simple. Even though I have multiple entries under the letter "C" (Christ, Christmas, Christians, etc.) an alphabetical filing system is much easier to use than a complicated, cross-reference system.

5) Acknowledge the source. Once you have written the illustration and title, record the source. Not only is it essential to know your source, but if you ever want to write for publication you will be asked to supply this information.

Next list the author's name, the book or article from which the illustration came, the publisher (and city), date, and page number where it appears. If the illustration was one you heard note as much information as you can: speaker's name, location, name of event, and date.

6) Quotes count too. Use your illustration file for quotable quotes. You have, no doubt, collected many throughout the years. Although it is difficult, give each quotation a title for cataloguing purposes. And don't forget to cite the source.

7) Mark the date and place of use. Need I say more? Once we've used an illustration, we certainly don't want to accidentally repeat it to the same people.

8) Pruning is helpful. Occasionally go through your illustration file and discard stories that appealed to you once but no longer seem valuable.

In the same way that frozen food can become stale over time, so can some of our "frozen stuff." Through regular pruning, you can cut down on the number of cards in your file. Reducing the excess bulk makes retrieval easier and more efficient. An added bonus is that the process of pruning helps recall what you have filed.

A word of warning—the illustration file is not the place to begin when writing a sermon. It can, however, be a source that sheds light on the topic about which we are writing or speaking.

GETTING READY TO PREACH

Bible study comes first. Later, if additional information is necessary to clarify a point, you can consult your illustration file. For example, a quick look under "Prayer," "Commitment," or "Stewardship," might result in just the right illumination for your sermon.

Remember to ask yourself two questions before using illustrations: "Does it fit?" and "Is it right for this setting?"

Illustration files serve several purposes. Not only are they helpful in preparing sermons, but also they provide a handy source of information for the many talks you are asked to give for groups, including Little League ball clubs, women's groups, civic groups, prayer breakfasts, dedications, the Red Cross, Fourth of July picnics, school gatherings, and the senior citizen organizations.

The Source for Illustrative Material

The sources of illustrative material are unlimited. They are everywhere—in our work, the newspapers, magazines, books, billboards, conversations, television, movies, lectures, sermons, and in the primary source, the Bible.

There are entire books of illustrations that have been catalogued and are ready for our use. Also there are illustration service companies that provide selected material on a regular basis.

Beyond all these sources is the ordinary all about us. Yogi Berra has reminded us, "You can see a lot just by looking." This secret explains some of the wisdom of Jesus' stories. He saw much meaning in the ordinary events of our lives.

You need not go out of your way to find them, just be alert to stories, sayings, thoughts, and experiences that speak to you. Dr. George Buttrick once remarked that reading for homiletical bits is an abomination. Dr. Halford Luccock warned his hearer years ago to never use stories or illustrations that others have used.

I disagree. There are stories and insights that belong to the world. Someone else may have discovered them first, but if they speak to you or bring light to a subject, use them.

Of course, we do not want to rely too heavily on sources from others. We need to become sensitive to ordinary things that can be woven into beautiful images. There is no shortage of material. As Jesus said, "He who has ears to hear, let him hear." And to this, I think he would add, "see."

Some may ask, "Do you gather illustrations even when you do not know how, when, where, or if they will be used? Yes. When I mark an illustration, a place for it may immediately come to mind; but most of the time, I am only recording something that piqued my interest. Most of what I have gathered will probably never be used, but I am not finished with my work yet. I still preach and speak and who knows what will be appropriate in the future.

I still collect interesting materials. There is rarely a day that some illustration is not marked for keeping. Uncovering mental images has been a lifelong quest for me, and I don't imagine it will ever end.

Although there is much value in having a filing system, at times there may be a temptation to become a slave to it. It is not the end, but a means to an end. It is a tool, and only a tool, to be used for constructive work. The value of a "system" such as the one described above lies in the ability to always be the master of the situation and not the slave.

Illustrative material is a valuable asset for the person that is constantly delivering sermons, speeches, and devotions. Finding, keeping, and being able to quickly uncover your material is a lifelong quest. The method you use will depend on your reading and workplace habits, and your organizational skills. Your task is to find the "system" that best fits your needs and then "do it."

Adapt a Filing System That Really Works!

The value of the filing cabinet comes from being a resource center for our daily work. It is the "keeping place" for your in-progress work as well as a storage place for the work that has been completed.

Properly organized and used, it houses the collection of our reading, thinking and planning. It is the gathering place for ideas, thoughts, papers, and articles that we will use. The repetitive nature of the seasons is an easy organizing principle that can be capitalized upon. For example, the resource section of your filing system could have the following five divisions: Holy Days/Seasons, Special Church Days, Civil Days, Prayers, and Miscellaneous.

Once these sections (and their subdivisions) have been created, then you have an appropriate place to store all those ideas, stories, articles, and worthwhile tidbits taken from many sources. Since it is nearly impossible to rely on our memories to find the source of that amusing story we read once, the filing cabinet is an excellent way to centralize the accumulation of all our work.

In my "Holy Days/Seasons" section of the filing cabinet, I label 14 separate hanging files as follows: Advent, Christmas Eve, Christmas Day, Epiphany, Lent, Ash Wednesday, Holy Week, Maundy Thursday, Passion/Palm Sunday, Easter, Pentecost, Christ the King, All Saints, and Reformation.

Your list may be longer or shorter, but one thing remains the same for all of us. No sooner do we breathe a sigh of relief that we have finished celebrating Easter, when it is time to do it again. And so it is with all the regular occasions in the year.

Thus, this repeating cycle of events should keep us in a continual state of preparation. It's always a good idea to save every usable idea we glean from personal devotions, Bible study, and other reading.

Then we won't find ourselves discovering great material or ideas and thinking, "I wish I had thought of this or known that when I preached during Lent last year." Guess what? Lent will be back before you know it, so make those files and start saving!

The "Special Church Days" section is subdivided into: Communion/Worldwide Communion Sunday, Ministry Sunday, Christian Education Sunday, Human Relations Day, Ecumenical Sunday, One Great Hour of Sharing, Native Awareness Sunday, Festival of the Christian Home, Peace with Justice Sunday, Bible Sunday, and Student Day.

Again, your subdivisions may differ, but be sure to include special conference days.

Some pastors pay close attention to civil calendars, and others disregard them altogether. However, since we are often called to speak at events in addition to preparing sermons, it is helpful to collect material on the national holidays—just in case.

Under "Civil Days," you may want to include: New Year, Martin Luther King Jr.'s Birthday, Mother's Day, Memorial Day, Father's Day, Independence Day, Labor Day, and Thanksgiving.

The "Prayers" section is a good place to keep track of prayers which have been collected from sources other than the liturgies of your church. These can be categorized as Confessions, Invocations, Offertory, Pastoral, and Benedictions.

The "Miscellaneous" section is a catch-all bin for anything worth keeping that doesn't fit any other category. This section continually expands and includes: Sermons from others, Sermons: Topics, Texts, Ideas, Thoughts/Ideas Worth Saving, For Ministers, Devotionals, Filler Material for Bulletins, Funeral Thoughts, and Stewardship Ideas.

As my responsibilities have changed through the years, the files have followed suit. As a bishop in the church, I now need files labeled Ordination Thoughts, Church Growth Plans, and Visioning. Adapt your miscellaneous section to fit your specific ministry needs.

Work in Progress: Create a Sermon Notebook

A sermon notebook can be any size or style. A simple three-ring binder works for many pastors. The advantage of an actual notebook is that it is portable. However, many pastors may prefer using a computer. Computers are advantageous because they offer significant storage capabilities and ease in adding and deleting material.

My sermon notebook began as a collection of notes for a series of sermons I wanted to preach. From the bookstores, I learned early in my ministry that many well-known pastors had written books of sermons on the Ten Commandments, the Apostles' Creed, the Beatitudes, the Lord's Prayer, and so forth.

Those books gave me the idea of creating my own notebook. In addition, it is helpful to make note of analogies from the Scriptures. The idea of exploring a series of sermons, on topics such as foundation, light, and salt, solves the problem of what to preach for two or even three months.

With a planned series on the Ten Commandments, for example, you can jot down notes in your notebook. Before long, one thought will lead to another, and you begin to explore numerous sermon possibilities in an informal way that will come in handy later.

Begin with ideas you have gleaned from titles in bookstores or previously read books. Then branch out to your own thoughts, such as a series on the parables of Jesus. List each on a separate page and go from there.

You may find that many other ideas for preaching emerge from unexpected sources or circumstances. Sometimes we read the Bible, spend time in devotion, visit the hospital, or converse with friends, and something jumps out at us crying to be preached.

During other times, Scriptures and ideas choose us. Make notes of all pertinent ideas in your sermon notebook.

Once a speaker referred to clergy as one of two types: squirrels or spiders. Spiders spin everything out of their insides while squirrels look for something to use, take it, and hide it for future use.

Why not be both? Some things we can discover and save. Other ideas emerge from within. Take advantage of both, and have a systematic way of recording everything in your own personal notebook.

A sign at a plant nursery said, "The best time to plant a tree is 15 years ago. The next best time is today." If there is nothing growing, plant something today.

A good place to begin is during preparation for teaching Bible study classes. Be sure to include your preparatory notes in your sermon notebook. Possible sermon texts constantly surface during those times. Why not let that research serve two purposes?

My sermon notebook really does remind me of a plant nursery in many ways because all my life I have found pleasure in taking cuttings from plants and rooting them.

At one time, I built my own greenhouse. Today, I have a garden dedicated to cuttings from many plants. As I prune the shrubs around my house, I take cuttings and stick them in the ground. With watering and some attention, cuttings take root. Signs of life don't happen overnight. All of the new plants do not develop, but many of them do.

A sermon notebook shows its owns signs of life after an adequate amount of time is spent planting cuttings from reading or thinking. Every week or two, read through your notebook to see what's there. Jot down any related ideas as you read.

In the small town where I grew up, I visited regularly an ever-flowing spring of water that bubbled forcefully from the ground. Regardless of how dry the parched earth was nearby, that spring always flowed.

Every pastor needs such a spring. We all know how it feels to work in the late hours and identify with the words of the disciples, "We have worked all night and caught nothing" (Luke 5:5).

I have preached for 46 years, and my notebooks are filled with material yet unpreached. Your notebook can be a spring that never runs dry, too!

C H A P T E R S I X

Blueprints for Preaching

Planning a preaching program is time consuming. It is a grueling, but exciting, week-long (or possibly longer) adventure. The block of time devoted to planning must be long enough and free from interruptions to allow a total spiritual saturation. For me it has often been an experience not unlike the time of Jesus with the disciples on the mountaintop.

At the beginning of my ministry, I did my planning work at home. This feat required the serious consideration of my family and my other responsibilities.

Later on I found I could accomplish this task much better if I withdrew from the local scene and "hid out" for seven to ten days. These days were totally consumed by hard work. Late summer proved to be the best time for me, but when and where you work will depend on you.

Option One: Design Based on Church Year

Most of us probably already follow the seasons of the church year sometimes. Even those of us who make little use of Epiphany, Holy Week, Trinity Sunday or even

Pentecost, usually feel the tugging of Christmas and Easter.

A few pastors just follow the leading of the Spirit. I hope all of us are led by that Spirit, but considering the major events in the life and ministry of Jesus, such as his birth, death, and resurrection, provides helpful guidance for our planning.

Preaching designed around the church year is a year-at-a-time quest. This option may work best for you, especially if you have difficulty making weekly decisions about what to preach. Regardless of the block of time you choose for your sermon planning, it helps to have the entire year in mind.

The first option is based on a year-long plan that basically follows the church year with attention given to other special times. The annual planning session begins with a calendar. Often we use one made up of Sundays and special days only, but because all preaching is not limited to Sundays, a full-scale calendar is better.

The first phase of planning is marking the seasons. How the seasons are designated varies from church to church and pastor to pastor. We are connectional, but local traditions and personal preferences play a major role in the planning for the seasons.

The seasonal blocks may include Advent, Christmastide, and Epiphany. In my planning, I attempt to use each of these seasons under a general umbrella covering themes, such as *coming* or *expectancy, arrival,* and *going.* You may prefer to break them apart and concentrate on Advent, Christmas, and Epiphany individually rather than as part of an entire season.

In some churches, the recognized season of the late fall and beginning of winter is Christmas. The banners of Advent and Epiphany may not be flying, but as the preacher, you can incorporate the emphases of these seasons into your preaching.

60

Regardless of the extent to which various seasons are recognized, observed, or celebrated by individual churches, it is important for your preaching plan to at least consider each season during which sermons will occur.

Another seasonal block is Lent. Following the conclusion of Epiphany, with its emphasis on manifestation, we are immediately catapulted into the time of preparation and spiritual awareness related to the crucifixion and resurrection of our Lord.

Beginning with Ash Wednesday, this six-week period moves deliberately toward the greatest of the Christian experience. The last week of Lent marks the last week of our Lord's life. Holy Week begins with Passion\Palm Sunday, moves through Maundy Thursday and Good Friday, and culminates with Easter, the celebration of the resurrection.

For many churches this season is the high point of the year. For others, the observance is almost totally a celebration of Easter. In either case, pastors can include themes dealing with Lent in their preaching plans.

Eastertide, a time for thinking about the post resurrection experiences of our Lord, begins immediately after Easter and continues until Pentecost.

This season is probably one of the least recognized for many congregations. Everyone knows it is the time following Easter, but few see it or keep it as a special time. In many churches, bulletins may carry the name of the season, and the church paraments display a different color from Lent, but it doesn't compare with the best known times of Christmas and Easter. Eastertide, however, offers the pastor a wealth of sermon possibilities.

Beginning with the day of Pentecost, we enter into that lengthy period of the same name marking the "letting loose" of the Holy Spirit upon the world. Many in the church have used Kingdomtide as a part of this season.

With the special day of Christ the King, the church year comes to an end.

The marking of the church seasons on the calendar is just the beginning of planning. Next, mark all the special times within each season.

Special days vary from church to church and pastor to pastor. First enter the general days, both holy and civil, that are generally recognized. Second, enter those days traditionally observed by your local congregation.

For example in my planning calendar, I mark all first Sundays as Communion days. All churches do not observe the Lord's Supper every first Sunday. A few offer communion every Sunday in a special service and only offer it at the "main" service during special times. Occasionally, I have not offered Communion on the first Sunday if the Christmas Eve communion service or the Maundy Thursday communion service has been near the first Sunday.

You don't need a communion sermon for every communion service, but when communion is offered, the sermon, whatever its theme, should lead toward this celebration.

Besides the special days already mentioned, the list can include: Christmas Eve, Watch Night, New Year, Human Relations Day, Martin Luther King Jr.'s Birthday, One Great Hour of Sharing, Mother's Day, Memorial Day, Father's Day, Independence Day, Labor Day, World Communion Day, Laity Day, Bible Sunday, and Thanksgiving Day.

Other days might include: Homecoming, Native American Awareness, Reformation, Ecumenical Sunday, Ministry Sunday, Student Day, Great Day of Singing, and Church Leadership Recognition.

When following the church year as the basis for preaching, you may want to consider planning either a series of sermons, a course of sermons, or both.

A series is a grouping of connected sermons. A course of sermons is a grouping of unrelated sermons that fit under a general theme.

For instance, drawing on Advent, Christmastide, and Epiphany, you could create a three-tiered course of sermons under the respective general theme. Similarly, Lent lends itself to a course of sermons.

During the summer season (certainly not a church season) when vacations are upon us, and church life is a bit less structured, I have often resorted to six or eight weeks of preaching on "lighter" subjects. For several years I used this time to preach on the general theme, "The Simple Truth," during which time, I spoke about the parables of Jesus.

The fall is a good time for a teaching ministry during which a pastor may speak for four or five weeks from a single book of the Bible. However, the busyness of fall becomes an obstacle to series-type preaching. Often, it seems that every Sunday demands a special emphasis.

After you have marked your calendar with seasons and special days, you are ready to enter individual sermon titles. How well you do this depends on the preparation you have made.

As has already been mentioned, I use the sermon notebook as a "sermonic mine" from which I can draw ideas. A sermon notebook alleviates the problem of finding something to preach; rather, you only have to figure out how to fit the sermons into the right places.

Most of us have several books of the Bible that we like to emphasize in our preaching. And there are themes that emerge from the Commandments, the Sermon on the Mount, the Beatitudes, the Parables, and the Lord's Prayer. The task of placement reminds me of working a jigsaw puzzle. You simply find the sermon piece that fits the season or theme with which you are working and direct it toward the needs of your congregation.

By the time I begin planning a year's worth of preaching, most of the sermon ideas in my notebook have been given one or more possible titles, a text, and a scripture. I choose the title and enter it on my calendar.

Keep in mind that you probably will not preach every Sunday, since you will take vacations, invite a lay person to speak on Laity Day, or host special guest preachers. Or perhaps you share the pulpit with an associate minister. Plan ahead.

Another suggestion is to use your sermon planning calendar to record hymn selections if you help choose the hymns in your church. These musical selections can support the themes of your sermons. Similarly, you may want to select other materials for worship, such as the Invocation, Call to Worship, or the Prayer of Confession, making them coincide with the sermon's theme.

Option Two: Design Based on the Lectionary

Today, the lectionary, selected scriptures arranged by dates, is used often and is a highly regarded resource for clergy and leaders of worship. If you are familiar with the wide selection of lectionary materials available, then you probably understand the breadth of its acceptance and use.

This has not always been the case. Twenty-five years ago, most clergy who attended Protestant seminaries were rarely exposed to the lectionary. It was used primarily by Roman Catholics and other highly liturgical groups.

The lectionary is not new. In the early centuries of the Christian tradition, it was used in churches. In fact, there were two lectionaries: one that *used the book-arrangement of the Bible as its base,* and the other that *planned scriptures according to the developing church year.* In Rome, the church-year lectionary plan became popular and has been used since.

The lectionary is a three-year arrangement of selected scriptures emphasizing the central message of the Bible. The plan follows the pattern of the church year that was developed from the life and ministry of Jesus. While there are some differences in the arrangement of the scriptures, the current lectionary has ecumenical roots and thus has found widespread use.

The lectionary is a selection of scriptures arranged so that the central message of the Bible is covered in three years. The three-year cycle is divided into three one-year series—A, B, and C. Each yearly series begins with Advent.

Each Sunday of the year is included in the lectionary, plus other generally celebrated holy days. Four scriptures are assigned for use on each Sunday: one from the Old Testament, the Psalms, an Epistle reading, and a reading from one of the Gospels. At the end of three years, the cycle is repeated.

Using the lectionary option as the basis for preaching planning is less demanding because the calendar has already been prepared. The church seasons and high, holy times are identified with appropriate scriptures.

I always relied on planning my own calendar until 1978, when I was appointed a district superintendent. Because my weekly preaching plan would be continually interrupted, I began working with the lectionary approach to sermon planning.

Setting Up the System

Organizing one's files according to the church seasons is one of the most efficient methods of establishing a systematic plan for sermon planning. Because the lectionary is based on a three-year cycle (A, B, and C), you can use three different colored folders to correspond with each year.

Assign one folder to each lectionary offering. When I first began doing this, I discovered that there are not 52, but 67 Sundays featured in the lectionary. Label each folder with the series letter, the number of the Sunday of the year, and the day being observed such as: **A-23 Fifth Sunday in Lent.**

On each file folder (not on the label), place an adhesive strip. Write on it the four selected scriptures for that day. (The scripture readings can also be placed in each folder, too, for quick access.)

The first reference index to the lectionary that I remember was *Seasons of the Gospels,* published in 1979 by Abingdon Press. This index lists every lection and is arranged by the books of the Bible.

For example, the scripture from Mark 2:1-12 is in the index with the information "15B," meaning the scripture is in the Gospel lection for the B year and the 15th day. Every lection of the three-year cycle is listed in this way.

The value of such an index is immeasurable, especially when I lead a Bible study class. After making notes for use when teaching the class, I file them in the appropriate lectionary folder. The index helps me locate this information quickly.

The same is true when preparing for teaching or leading a Sunday school class, confirmation group, or Disciple Bible Study group. The pastor's life is filled with reading and rereading the scriptures. One's devotional time centers in Bible readings. The lectionary index and file allows work to be saved for the appropriate season.

When I began my lectionary work, there were few materials available. Whenever I discovered a new resource I tore it apart and placed the material in the appropriate folder. With the explosion of lectionary materials now available, it would take a box to hold them all. Many of them are extremely useful, but nothing takes the place of your own research.

With the lectionary file now stocked with thoughts and ideas from a variety of sources, no Sunday comes without a place to begin. All the gathered material will not be used; but don't despair, a new cycle will again come around.

Weigh Your Choices: Pros and Cons

To help determine which plan is right for you, consider the following pros and cons of each.

Option One: Design Based on the Church Year

Pros:

1) Gives a sense of direction for the entire year.
2) Avoids the weekly question, "What am I going to preach on next Sunday?"
3) Avoids riding a "hobbyhorse" in preaching.
4) Undergirds and supports the work that others are doing.
5) Encourages disciplined study and reading.
6) Adds zest, excitement, and anticipation to sermon preparation.
7) Relieves stress and anxiety.

Cons:

1) In areas where the lectionary is commonly used and study groups have been formed, this type of planning may not be useful. (For those who do not follow the lectionary, staying abreast of the cycle could prove beneficial. The multitude of lectionary material that is available provides valuable knowledge and assistance in sermon planning.)
2) Special concerns and general church matters are difficult to accommodate. Once you have planned a year's worth of preaching, detours are difficult. Altering your course frequently detracts from the continuity you hope to provide.

Option Two: Design Based on the Lectionary

Pros:
1) Provides a solid base for using the entire Bible as a resource for preaching. (This method exposes the congregation to the entire Bible, not just those sections that interest the pastor.)
2) Demands a disciplined study of the Bible.
3) Avoids riding "hobbyhorses."
4) Offers the possibility of integrating the sermon with the liturgy of the worship experience. (This can be accomplished through other plans also, but the lectionary is a good way of doing it.)
5) Opens the door for peer groups to have a common ground for Bible study and sermon discussions.
6) Places the church into the ecumenical sphere of liturgy and preaching.

Cons:
1) Can become a crutch that stifles creative preaching.
2) The availability of materials presents the temptation to rely too heavily on the thinking and study of others.
3) Often excludes the special and traditional days which are celebrated in the local congregation.
4) Denominational emphases are often difficult to work into the sermon.
5) Does not always lend itself to series or special theme preaching.

Inspect Your Work

Regardless of the plan you choose to follow, once you have successfully completed your sermon blueprint ask yourself these questions:

BLUEPRINTS FOR PREACHING

- Is my preaching program supportive of the church's vision and goals?

- Is my preaching supporting the work being done by those involved in education, evangelism, missions, stewardship, and other program units of the church?

- Is my preaching engaging the congregation in the endeavors that characterize Christianity?

- Is my preaching doing anything about the cries and hurts of the congregation?

- Can the sermons listed on my calendar be made relevant?

- Is my preaching supportive of the General Church and Annual Conference emphases?

- Is my preaching adequately supporting the teaching opportunities of the pulpit?

After answering these questions honestly, scrutinize your calendar. Some reshuffling may need to take place. Make the necessary adjustments and changes.

When the calendar has been filled, it is time to move to the sermon file folders. A folder is made for each sermon listing the title and the proposed date for use on the tab.

Deposit the gathered material from the notebook or lectionary file in each folder. In some cases, the basic parts of the sermon will have already been written. Some will have little more than a text and a page or two of thoughts about the subject. In either case, place it in the appropriate file.

This file folder now becomes the reservoir for every new thought and idea you discover. Regularly peruse it. Knowing the sermon subjects for the next year is a powerful force in finding material and weaving ideas from your thoughts and prayers into your planning process. You will find a story, illustration, or idea always cropping up.

Unveil Plans to Coworkers

It's a good idea to share your blueprint with others. One way is on separate sheets of paper list every Sunday of the year, from Advent to Advent. On each sheet write the sermon title, text, scripture, hymns, and a descriptive sentence about the theme for the day.

Share these sheets with the church staff—professional and support—and with anyone responsible for worship or others whose work would be helped by having them.

One group often overlooked in this process is the committee that prepares the flowers. A creative altar group can sometimes do wonders with flowers and other materials if they know the theme of the day ahead of time.

Finally, consider attaching a cover letter, similar to the one on page 71, to your sheet.

These blueprint suggestions may not be the right ones for you. That's all right. The point is to have some type of plan and work at it.

There is much more to being a herald of the Lord's work than developing a preaching plan and having a well organized system. At best it is only a means to an end. It is the nuts and bolts of holding some things together. Whatever the plan, good preaching will come only from prolonged periods with the Lord, faithful study, a keen awareness of the world of the congregation and good communication skills.

To all supporting team members of XYZ church:

The following pages represent an attempt to share the preaching program of XYZ church. The sermon title is given, the text, scripture lesson, and a brief description of the subject. Suggested hymns are also included.

This preaching schedule does not represent a "fixed-in-stone" program. At best, it is only a direction. There will be times when the community or world situation will demand an immediate word. At that time, the schedule sermon topic will be altered.

There may be times when I or we feel God is moving us in other directions. I want to always be open to that leading. Since the sermons listed here are not finished products, what once appeared to be a worthwhile sermon may not prove worthy of delivery. In some instances a better title will be uncovered and used.

This preaching program has been planned with the mission and vision of this church, the special emphases of the United Methodist Church, and the interest of all the work being done in this congregation in mind. My constant hope is that the XYZ pulpit will be a teaching arm of the church and a prophetic voice will be heard from it. It is my prayer and hope that this information will be helpful to all of you.

Preaching must never simply reflect a consensus, but your comments and suggestions concerning the preaching program will be appreciated.

Sincerely,
Your Pastor

CHAPTER SEVEN

Preparing to Build a Sermon

Many people in our congregations probably think preachers study and practice the art of sermon preparation the same way that a surgeon studies and practices surgical procedures. Seminaries are currently doing a better job of teaching these skills; however, regardless of how much a student learns, the sermon requires far more than the simple repetition of writing skills.

My seminary training provided an excellent foundation in theology, ancient language, church history, biblical studies, comparative religions and many other academic subjects. I appreciated those studies, but my education did not adequately equip me to prepare sermons.

My first congregation had no idea how little I knew about the art of preaching. I learned by doing—trial and error.

Preparation for preaching is a mixture of everything the pastor does. The academic background studies, the relationship with the congregation, the involvement in the community, the administration of the church, personal devotional time, the continual reading of periodicals and books—all of these contribute to preaching. Sermons are not developed or delivered in a vacuum or outside of one. The sermon comes from many streams of thought and work.

This chapter focuses on the preparation of the written sermon.

Steep Yourself in Bible Reading

Facing a blank sheet of paper or computer screen is foreboding. You can almost hear the words, "I dare you! I dare you!" Sometimes it is easier to move a fallen tree from across a road than it is to face a blank sheet of paper or an empty screen.

How do we prepare to begin? If we follow either the lectionary or church year plan which are described in chapter 6, then we at least have an idea: a scripture, a text, a collection of thoughts. This collection of ideas can be compared to a jumper cable to start the mental engine.

The best preparation begins with steeping yourself in the scriptures. I once heard a story about a rabbi who was walking down the street when a member of his congregation came along boasting that he had read all the volumes of the Talmud three times. The rabbi looked at him and said, "The important thing is not how many times you have been through the Talmud, but whether the Talmud has been through you."

When we have our sermon idea, we benefit by living with the scriptures, not just reading them. We can become a participant in whatever is happening.

Use a Bible atlas to visit the place and journey with the people. If Jesus is traveling from Capernaum to Nazareth and on to Jerusalem, join him in making the trip. Experience the miles of travel and the villages on the way.

Look into the shops as you pass, see the people in the streets, smell the odors from the stables, speak to the people standing in line at the community well. If you look carefully, you can see the sheep, the olive groves, and the laborers harvesting the crop.

Be present with the woman of Bethany as she bursts into the room to anoint Jesus with oil. No woman about to throw expensive oil on the Lord will casually walk into the room. She bursts through the door. Listen to the door as she slams it. Watch every step, see the excitement in her face, observe her emotions, and experience the electricity in the air.

Live with Peter following the betrayal on the night of Jesus' arrest. Can you see the disappointment on his face? What did he say to the others? Where did he go?

Or perhaps the scripture you are reading is about Barabbas being set free. Where do you suppose he went? Did he return to his old ways, taking up his trade of being a fiery revolutionary? Did he leave the country and never return? Was he later arrested?

In the story of the feeding of the five thousand, what kind of conversation took place among the disciples? Can you see the amazement on the faces of the people? What happened after the feeding? What kinds of stories were later told in the villages about the experience? "Penetrate the scriptures until they yield up its treasure," says John R. W. Stott.[1] God, when speaking to Ezekiel, asked him to "eat the scroll": "He said to me, O mortal, eat what is offered to you; eat this scroll, and go, speak to the house of Israel. So I opened my mouth, and he gave me the scroll to eat. He said to me, Mortal, eat this scroll that I give you and fill your stomach with it. Then I ate it; and in my mouth it was as sweet as honey" (Ezekiel 3:13).

Just as we soak our bodies in a hot tub of water, we must also soak our minds with the scriptures. As blood flows through our bodies, so must the Bible flow through our spirits. It is not enough to make a casual foray into the Bible in search of a few ripe morsels of fruit that can be plucked for Sunday's sermon. This soaking is like an incubation period, a time of awaiting a new birth of truth.

Stott said we should "probe the text, like a bee with a spring blossom, or like a humming bird probing a hibiscus flower for its nectar. Worry at it like a dog with a bone. Suck it as a child sucks an orange. Chew it as a cow chews the cud."

C. H. Spurgeon adds we must read the word "as a worm bores its way into the kernel of the nut."

The Bible must be studied expectantly. We must read as expectantly as the person who pans for gold. Read and study, believing something will be revealed as Moses did: "Show me your glory, I pray." (Exod. 33:18) or Samuel: "Speak, LORD, for your servant is listening" (I Sam. 3:9).

Apply a Crowbar to the Scriptures

Cultivating a historical imagination is important for an effective preacher. This skill begins with the process of becoming a participant, and it progresses to asking several questions:

Who is the central spokesperson and what are his\her credentials?

If the word is from God, then who is the herald of it? Is it one of the prophets or apostles? Is it Jesus?

What is the situation that prompted the author to speak? There is much history and narrative in the Bible, and most of it is there for a purpose.

Who are the people to whom the words are addressed? Where do they live? What is their history? What is their religious tradition?

What is the mood of the people? Are they suffering from a loss of hope? Are they struggling as exiled

people? Are they excited about the future? Is their
way of living being questioned?

What is the central message? What is the focus of
the story or event? Is it clear? Can it be told in a
sentence or two?

Does the story speak to needs today? Is there a need
that may be met by my preaching from this passage?

Do not answer these questions as you would respond to
a survey. The particular scripture you are considering will
determine which questions are pertinent. The object of
this wrestling with the scripture is to clarify the situation
and the meaning—for the first-time hearers and for the
congregation.

Such in-depth study of the scripture will produce
mountains of material, too much, in fact, to share with
the congregation. Your aim is not to impress them with
your scholarly research, but to use your study as a foundation for the sermon.

Measure Your Audience

Consider your congregation as your anticipated audience. Who are they and what are their needs?

Borrowing a marketing term, clergy frequently talk
about "targeting." They ask themselves, "Who am I trying
to reach with this sermon?" Is there an identifiable group
that this sermon can be directed toward?

Some pastors are appalled at the thought of separating
a congregation into groups and targeting sermons toward
certain segments. The objection to this concept is that all
are there to be fed spiritually, and no one should be left
out. Others see targeting as a currently popular marketing
strategy which is destined to fade away as so many new
ideas do.

However, identifying hearers is not a new idea. Targeting the sermon is as old as the first pronouncements of the

Lord. The judges and the prophets spoke to the needs of particular groups. There were very few "to whom it may concern" addresses.

Jesus was a master at targeting his words. He spoke to a particular group with particular needs. His words had timeless merit, but in context, they were spoken to certain people.

Our American religious history is filled with stories about the camp meetings and evangelistic gatherings where people gathered for days or weeks to hear the word. The sermons delivered from those makeshift pulpits targeted "sinners." The sermons were prepared for those people and delivered with gusto and power.

Some churches target "seekers." The sermon is aimed toward those who are seeking something they do not have. Others target "decision making." They call for people to make a decision to accept Christ (much like the old camp meetings did). Still others focus on spiritual formation or maturing in the Christian faith.

I asked the pastor of a church where I served as preacher for a four-day mission event, several questions about his congregation: Where were they in their ministry? What type of people would probably be present? and What was their relationship to the church?

He replied that the people most likely to attend were fairly active in the church and probably long-term members who made up the core of the congregation.

His final comment was, "I hope you will prepare sermons that help them mature in their discipleship responsibilities and do more for Christ than simply show up at church events." With this information, I was in a much better position to craft my sermons. This is targeting.

In most congregations on a typical Sunday morning, we have a variety of persons present. There are usually a few seekers, and also several people who should be making decisions for Christ or deeper commitments.

We have some who have been lifelong members and are fairly content with who they are and what they are doing. Hopefully, there are a few others who desire help in moving forward toward more meaningful discipleship responsibilities. The sermon should offer help to all these people, but having some group in mind as the sermon is being prepared will give you a sense of direction.

The pastor now has the sermon nugget which includes all of the accumulated thoughts, the gleanings from a careful study of the scriptures, and a feel for the audience. It's time to move on.

CHAPTER EIGHT

Starting Construction

Chisel a Focal Point

The first step in writing a sermon is to chisel out a clear phrase that represents the focus of the sermon. It will probably not be a part of the sermon itself, but it clearly charts the direction of the sermon. This focus should be stated in one or two sentences. It is a statement of intent.

A lawyer appearing before the Supreme Court stands before the judges and states the intent of the argument that is to come: "I propose to show that . . ." and in a brief sentence sets forth the intentions of the case. This one- or two-sentence statement which was given to the court may have taken hours or days to fully unfold, but the proposal is succinctly stated.

It is no different with a sermon. For my own benefit, I write at the top of the page, "The object of this sermon is to . . ." This distilled and clearly stated goal becomes my road map.

Archbishop Whately said of a preacher, "He aimed at nothing, and hit it."[1] Keep your eye focused on your object. Your written statement also serves to prevent adding extraneous topics to your sermon.

Overloaded airplanes cannot leave the runway; over-loaded sermons cannot fly either. A clear intent will give wings to your sermon.

Option One: Hammer an Outline

There is no single, proven way to write. Temperaments and work styles are so different that each person must accommodate their unique preferences into their writing practices.

At the start of a pastor's ministry, many attempt to copy another person's style. We can learn from each other, of course. Eventually though, everyone finds the method that is right for him or her. After all, Erasmus, a sixteenth century Dutch scholar and teacher, said "If elephants can be trained to dance, lions to play, and leopards to hunt, surely preachers can be taught to preach."[2]

There are several different sermon structures. At least five types have been identified. The expository sermon follows one structure. The narrative follows another. The ladder sermon uses upward or downward rungs. The jewel approach examines a sermon idea from all sides. The blaze of glory sermon, in which a skyrocket is quickly launched and followed, demands something different.

Regardless of the chosen structure, you may want to follow the outline approach to writing. In some English composition classes, nothing is written until it has been outlined.

Once the outline is completed, writing begins. Some people live by this rule and will not approach a writing assignment without a full outline.

Occasionally, the collected material will be such that a general outline will quickly surface. At other times, the basic structure is more elusive.

Many pastors fall into the rut of using the same structure again and again. We have all heard about the basic form—three points and a poem.

As the body is built around and held in place by the skeleton, there must also be a frame that holds together the material of a sermon. The frame is the central theme.

Currently, there is great variety in the structure of sermons. The text does not always demand the structure, but often it does speak to the way in which the sermon should be organized. The structure of the sermon should unfold from the scripture like a flower unfolds from its bud.

Option Two: Prime the Pump by Writing

The starting point for most of us is to just start writing. "Writing what?" some might ask. The first sentence. It is difficult, but for that reason, sometimes it is easiest to start writing anything that comes to mind.

Usually with this technique, you will write sentences that are not important and will later be discarded, but at least you will be forced to begin. I am always amazed when I use this process to discover that from somewhere, a sermon begins to emerge.

This practice primes the mental pump. As a young boy, I lived near an old pump with a big, long handle. Before we could get any water from the well, we had to pump the handle several times.

Writing is no different than pumping water. This simple act of priming uncaps the mind and allows the creative juices to flow.

Sometimes the creative waters lead me down a path that seems contrary to my destination, but I follow it anyway. Strangely enough, those unexplored paths sometimes lead me into new directions that give the sermon an unexpected shape.

Writing also gives us a chance to massage the material and to be massaged by it. Once while watching a potter at a craft fair, I saw him add clay, and wetting it now and then, he began to play with it

I asked, "What are you going to make?" To my surprise, he answered, "I don't know yet. Right now, I'm simply trying to get a feel for the material. In a few minutes, it will tell me."

I am far from being a mystic, but writing one's reflections and thoughts—even random ones—has a mysterious quality. Thoughts often rise up and begin to speak.

How far you get with your writing depends upon the material, your familiarity with it, and how long you stay with it. Occasionally, you will complete a rough draft of the sermon. At other times, you will just assimilate a continuing collection of ideas and thoughts. Keep writing, however, until your inspiration is exhausted.

Framing

The body of the sermon is the heart of the message and usually is the first to be written. However, there are two other extremely important parts: the introduction and the conclusion. They are vital to a good sermon and both demand one's best effort.

Introductions—Regardless of whether you use the outline method or the prime the pump writing method described above, make sure your introduction is attention grabbing.

One of the most difficult sentences to write is the first one. Composing those first few words is like taking an initial plunge into an old swimming hole in a cold creek. You have to psyche yourself up and do it.

The purpose of the introduction is twofold. First, it captures the attention of the listeners, arouses interest, stimulates curiosity, and whets the appetite.

Second, it introduces the theme. It is usually easy to do one of these, but to do both requires creativity. Often the exposition of the text becomes the opening. At other times, a well-chosen illustration or story may become the opening.

Conclusions—If launching into the writing of a sermon is difficult, then bringing it into port is no easier. When you learn to ride a bicycle, one of the most difficult tasks is learning to get off.

It seems strange that we have trouble ending sermons, but we do. Sometimes we are like buzzards, circling around and around, not quite knowing how to land.

The conclusion of a sermon should be a call, and an expectation of something to happen. Jesus made it clear that we should be "doers of the word, and not merely hearers" (James 1:22). John Wesley spoke often about the sermon going from the mind and into the heart.

The nature of the call or expectation will depend upon the intent of the sermon, but it should be clear and precisely stated with a mobilizing quality. This is the "wrap-up" that the attorney delivers before the jury. All the previous work is on the line. This is the moment when decisions are going to be made.

Detailing

The great preacher W. E. Sangster said, "Illustrations are windows that let the light into a sermon." They are to the sermon.what the glass openings are to our houses. They bathe the interior with light so that one may see more clearly.

Similarly, Aristotle said, "The mind never thinks without a picture." The words we read, or thoughts we have received into our minds, are immediately translated into an image. It is the newly received picture that becomes the basis of our understanding. We see with our minds as well as our eyes.

Jesus is the best example we have of teachers and preachers using mental pictures. He constantly made a connection between a well-known and understood idea or event to a truth. We call his mental pictures parables.

GETTING READY TO PREACH

The dictionary defines a parable as "a short simple story told for the purpose of teaching a moral lesson." Jesus used easily grasped ideas to illustrate important truths.

The vine, salt, laborers in the fields, sowing seeds, and harvesttime were some of his favorites. His pictures were often brief but opened the mind in a marvelous way: "A city built on a hill cannot be hid. No one after lighting a lamp puts it under a bushel basket" (Matt. 5:14).

The images Jesus used included: children playing in the marketplace, a robbery along a road, a woman sewing, and the loss of some coins.

Some parables were longer than others, such as "A sower went out to sow . . ." These mental images were not used for entertainment or to convey what he knew, but for the purpose of opening a window to an important truth.

The parable or illustrative picture is a basic ingredient for communication. No one knows this better than the preacher who struggles week after week to clearly communicate. The saying, "A picture is worth a thousand words," is quoted often because it is true.

When we artistically paint pictures with words they come alive to listeners. Illustrations open the mind and stir the imagination. They help the listeners see as well as hear. They illuminate the subject.

There are a few persons, I hope only a few, that frown on using illustrations of any kind. Most of us, however, have learned their value and use them wherever and whenever we can. Often an ordinary sermon will be redeemed by one good mental picture or story, and it is the story or illustrative thought that causes the truth we are communicating to be remembered. The truth finds a lodging place.

Ten Checkpoints

✓ Use only illustrations that fit your congregation and yourself. Unless you both have a knowledge of opera, it is best not to use it as a source of "picture" material. In certain situations, the same is true of art or literature subject matter.

Similarly, a vivid illustration about the milking hour on a dairy farm may be beyond the comprehension of some congregations. Although some of the people will understand your meaning, the majority of them may not. Unless you can effectively make your point using non-familiar sources, leave them alone.

✓ Use only illustrations that clearly relate to the truth being presented and shed light upon it. People often use accent lights around plants and throughout their dwellings for the purpose of enhancement. The lights have no value in and of themselves.

All of us have heard illustrations that were thrown in to enliven the presentation. There is a time for stories to be told for the sake of the story, but that activity is unrelated to the work of sermon writing.

Avoid the temptation to chisel an illustration in order to make it fit your sermon. Leave it alone until it speaks its own truth. The time will come for it later.

✓ Use illustrations sparingly enough that the truth is not lost by too many windows. Sometimes we are tempted to string several good stories and quotes together in order to avoid boredom. These stories and quotes may be interesting, but ask yourself, "Is there a purpose to these?" If the answer is no, don't use them.

It is possible to use so many illustrations that they take center stage instead of enhancing or illuminating the central theme of the sermon. As you write, pay close attention to the number and types of illustrations used.

✓ Use illustrations that are in good taste for the occasion. Make sure the stories you use are not offensive to anyone. We have come a long way in our understanding and appreciation of diversity. Even though there may be no one in the congregation who would be personally injured, some have friends and relatives from different backgrounds and heritages. A story told at another's expense is often an explosive experience.

✓ Cite the source of illustrations used if they are taken from other sources. If the illustration did not arise from personal experience always give the source. If it is a story that just seems to make the rounds, it is appropriate to say, "I heard a story about . . ." However, if possible, say something more specific, such as "Dr. Robert Spain told about an experience . . ." or "In the book titled XYZ, author Dr. Robert Spain tells about . . ." It doesn't detract from the window to credit someone else's revealing thought.

✓ Avoid using illustrations from confidential conversations from the past or present. Although no one in your congregation may know the persons involved, they will be less likely to place trust in you. No one wants to think his problems will be aired in the pulpit.

✓ Utilize personal family illustration sparingly and with care. All of us occasionally bring our families into our preaching. Such illustrations are often appropriate and appreciated. My grandchildren are a great source of stories. Most congregations enjoy hearing tidbits that are family related, but remember that overuse of such material negates the intended effect.

STARTING CONSTRUCTION

✓ Avoid building a sermon around an illustration. This is comparable to a builder who builds a house around a coveted fireplace mantel. The illustration is not the place to begin. All of us have a few prize stories that we would like to share, but they must not become the sermon. Remember the illustration must always play the supporting role.

✓ Resist illustrating what is already clear. There are some truths or ideas that are so clear and so well known that they need no further work. Even if you intend to use a choice illustration, do not yield to the temptation.

A law professor was fond of telling the students, "At the moment the jury is convinced of your evidence, say no more."

✓ Refrain from using illustrations that require an explanation. A lamp doesn't have to be explained, and neither does a window. They should stand alone.

The only limitation to available material is personal preferences. Some pastors frown on using anything from a newspaper or certain magazines. Others refuse to use material from a "canned" source, such as illustration books. Many preachers rely almost exclusively on illustrations from the Bible.

I have few qualms about any legitimate resource. The rationale for me is not where the material comes from but whether it fits the checkpoints listed above.

Tighten and Polish Your Language

All of us do not possess the same vocabulary skills, but we must develop the best use of words that we can. Sermons do not have to be filled with multisyllable words, but do use words that are clear, concise, and colorful. Cultivate the use of picture words, those that paint mental pictures.

My computer has a software program that scores the level of my writing in a document. Most books are currently written between grade school and high school levels. Occasionally I use my software program to check the reading level of my sermons. However, regardless of the reading level of the sermon, the word choices are important.

A preacher once quoted Mark Twain as having said that the difference between using the right word and the nearly right word is the difference between lightning and the lightning bug.

Allow Setting Time

While the writing has been shaping the structure of the sermon, the entire work is not usually completed at one time.

The sermon needs some incubation time. Like yeast in dough, your own thoughts need time to transform the sermon. This waiting time allows the spirit working through the subconscious to continue the work while you are involved in other activities. When you return to the sermon, you may find that new ideas on the subject have surfaced.

Time away from the sermon is a valuable, creative experience. Returning later to reread what was previously written usually produces new insights. Then rewriting continues. By now the scriptures and a mental picture of your audience begin to come together. In the same way the ingredients of a recipe combine to create a delicious dish, your sermon is being created.

Each of us is different, but I find that my sermons are not usually finished until the time of preaching is near. By "near," I don't mean the Saturday night before Sunday morning, but sometime about a month or so before I use them.

Pruning Time

By this time, there will usually be more new growth than one can use in any single sermon. Pruning is never easy. It's hard to cut away what appears to be good branches, but it must be done. You must be ruthless in discarding those things that are not directly relevant to the subject. A common complaint about sermons is that there is too much material in one sermon. Go ahead! Cut away everything, even some good material, that doesn't directly fit the established intent of the sermon.

The pruned material does not have to be discarded. At my home, I have a small garden spot where I plant the prunings from shrubs and perennial plants. With watering and care, many of these clippings will take root and new plants will emerge. It is no different from the prunings of your writing. The pruned material (if it appears to be useful) should be planted in the appropriate notebook or file for possible new rootings. It is amazing what these new roots sometimes produce.

Now that the sermon is constructed, it's time to review your work.

CHAPTER NINE

Evaluating Your Work

A well-written sermon is not a guarantee of good preaching, because there is still the matter of communication. However, crafting a good draft of the sermon is a beginning and a key component.

Few accomplishments are more enjoyable for a pastor than finishing a sermon that he or she feels good about. The struggle and tough work seem to be worth it all. A well-written sermon gives the preacher confidence in the material and creates excitement for the preaching experience.

After the sermon has been written, the evaluating phase begins. Ask yourself the following questions:

- Have the scriptures been used honestly?
- Have I maintained my intended focus?
- Does the sermon offer help for hurting people?
- Does the sermon have movement?
- Is each point and idea clearly presented?
- Do the illustrations act as windows to add understanding?
- Is the response expectation clear?

These questions, along with others you will ask, may cause you to reconsider parts of your sermon.

It is helpful to continue the evaluation process even after the sermon has been preached. Have someone videotape your sermon, and then watch it with a select group of people or alone. These sessions are much like a football coach with the staff reviewing previous games. Every bit of the worship service can be viewed to see what did and did not happen.

When I watch my sermons on tape, I ask the following questions:

- Did the introduction capture the congregation's attention?

- Did I make God's Word live?

- Did the sermon connect with the people?

- Did I make clear the expectation of the sermon?

- Did the sermon move toward the conclusion?

Your questions may differ from mine, but the answers you receive are important for future sermons.

Seven Hallmarks of Effective Preaching

I was once informed by a church pastor/parish committee that they wanted a change in pastoral leadership. The group claimed the present pastor couldn't preach. They also shared with the pastor what they had said to me.

Later during a conversation with the pastor, I asked about his preaching. He replied, "Those people wouldn't know a good sermon if they heard one."

What constitutes good preaching? What are the marks of effective preaching?

1. Effective preaching must reflect a knowledge of God.
At a ministers conference a bishop talked about a church that needed a Sunday school teacher for a youth class. A young theological student, home for the summer, was asked to be the teacher. He agreed, and when he arrived the following Sunday morning, he was greeted by eight or ten students.

Sitting on the edge of a table, he looked them over and asked, "Well, what would you like to talk about?" There was dead silence. No one moved. He repeated the question, and still no one uttered a word.

With even more gusto, he asked, "What would you like to talk about?" Finally, a young girl broke the silence by asking, "What do you know something about?"

It was a good question. Do we know about God? Can we speak about God out of the accumulation of 3000 years of history? Do we know the working of God in the world?

Unfortunately, a quotation in *Fortune* magazine may reflect a common opinion toward the church, "What we of the world need is a word from God and we look to the church for that word . . . and all we hear is the echo of our own voice."

Lest we think this quotation is unique, consider the words of Henry R. Luce, editor of *Time-Life Books*, "We are thirsty for the truth! We are bored by stale moralisms and inept attempts to comment constantly on current affairs. Do you know anything about God? That's what we in the church and out of it want to know. Can you tell us something about God?"

The people who come to our churches are crying out for some word from the Lord. They may not clearly express it, but they are looking, sometimes unknowingly, for something that will sustain them.

Augustine spoke of the restlessness of the soul. That restlessness is a part of our world, and a part of many of

EVALUATING YOUR WORK

the people who listen to our preaching. We can't give them something that we don't have.

When we go to a physician or an attorney, we expect to find a knowledgeable, well-prepared person in his or her field. It is no different with us. We cannot know everything, but we had better be sure we are well grounded in our knowledge about God.

Thomas Merton, in *Seven Storey Mountain*, an autobiography of a man's search for faith, tells about going to his grandfather's Zion church:

"The minister was called Mr. Riley. Pop always called him Dr. Riley. He was always friendly to me and used to get into conversation about intellectual matters and modern literature. It seems that he counted much on this sort of thing. He considered this to be an essential part of his ministry and somehow believed this was what the people came to church to hear.

"It was always literature and politics that he talked about, not religion and God. You felt the man did not know his vocation, did not know what he was supposed to be. He had taken upon himself some function in society which was not his and which was not necessarily a function at all."

This quotation could be misunderstood by some as suggesting that literature and the happenings of the world are not important. They are, and preachers (as well as everyone else) should be well informed about world matters. But Thomas Merton went to church in the hope of hearing something from God.

Our people have a right to expect good preaching to reflect a knowledge of God.

2. Effective preaching must reflect a personal relationship with God through Jesus Christ.

The Bible is a history of God's work with people to fulfill the dream for the world. We are a part of that

93

unfolding dream. Knowing about God is important, but knowing God personally is something else altogether. We must be so close to God that the people will see God at our elbow the entire time we are in the pulpit.

The preacher's function is analogous to the relationship between the moon and the sun. The moon reflects light from the sun. Our sermons need to reflect the light that comes from God so that the whole world may be spiritually bathed and nourished. This result will not occur unless we are near enough to God to see and feel the light.

How is your prayer life? Do you spend enough time reflecting on God and letting God fill you?

Martin Luther once said, "I have so many things to do today that I shall have to spend several hours in prayer." We need extended times in prayer. People who have no fresh word from the Lord cannot bring anything fresh from him to others.

The church in Korea, a modern Christianity success story, points to prayer as the reason behind the success. The people spend hours in prayer, beginning each morning either in church or at home praying.

Reading and studying is a valuable part of the ministers daily habits, but one's prayer life is essential. If our preaching is to reflect God, then we must be very close to the light. The closer we are, the wider the reflection.

3. Effective preaching must open the veil upon God.

As in the temple at the crucifixion of Jesus, good preaching must rip open the veil of the Holy of holies for the people. It must let the people see God, and not the preacher. The spotlight must never be allowed to illuminate us, but God.

While Dr. Halford Luccock was serving as the preacher for a mission group in New York, a lay person is said to have led this prayer, "O Lord, we thank Thee for our brother. Now blot him out! Reveal Thy glory to us in such blazing splendor that he shall be forgotten."

Once I heard Brian Green from England preach and then lecture on preaching. Afterwards a young clergy asked, "Dr. Green, how can I learn to be a great preacher?"

He replied, "When you are in the pulpit, visualize a huge cross right behind you. Then get out of the way and let the people see it." Effective preaching allows people to catch a glimpse of God.

4. Effective preaching must reflect a "caring" for people.

Andre Crouch, the gospel songwriter and musician, was at the pinnacle of his career churning out hit songs when he received a letter from his father that said, "When you make it to the top, don't forget that all that really matters are people. When you stop having a burden for people, then it is time for you to come home."

We are to introduce people to the Lord, to nurture them in Christian love and turn them out into the world as living witnesses. We must reclaim a passion for the people for whom Christ died. The people in our congregations are not there to serve us. We are to serve them, and a part of serving is caring.

Caring for people is expressed in more ways than preaching a sermon, but caring must be shown here, too. People can tell when we care. Caring is reflected even when judgments are proclaimed or hope is offered. It is reflected through facial expressions, the tone of the voice, speech rhythms, and even in deliberate pauses. It is as easy to spot caring in preaching as it is to spot caring in a visit to the bereaved.

Preaching must be much more than a rote recitation— even when profound truths are proclaimed. Caring must be expressed in everything we do. It is a part of good preaching.

5. Effective preaching must offer expectancy and hope.
Robert Louis Stevenson kept a diary during his life. After his death, portions of the diary were made public. One interesting entry read, "I went to church today . . . and am not depressed." Apparently he was so surprised that he made note of it.

Every congregation has hurting people. We know about many of them, but often we are unaware of many hurts and disappointments. So for everyone, the sermon must be a spring of spiritual water bathing their wounds. It must be the first crocus of spring, announcing the surge of new life. The sermon must lift live coals from God's fire and show people how to light their own fires from it.

There are, of course, times when God identified wrong and disappointment in the people and spoke directly to them about it. The same will be true for any preacher with a prophetic voice, but we don't have to leave listeners with their misspent or mismanaged lives.

That's the glory of the good news. There is a way out. Sin is all about us. It is rampant in our society, but Jesus gave us a way to break out of it. However dark we may paint a picture, somewhere turn the light on and let the people at least see the hope—even when they do not accept it.

What runway lights are at night to a plane, the gospel should be to those struggling with darkness. What a parachute is to the person making his or her first jump, the word from the Lord should be to those who are anxious or nervous about the future.

Jesus never left people without offering them life—real life. Is it asking too much for us to do the same?

6. Effective preaching must lead toward a verdict.
The sermon must be more than information. We must lead people to do something about the topic we are preaching about, and we must expect a change to take place.

One of the saddest letters I received as a bishop came from a woman writing about her preacher. She said he was a good pastor, a good preacher, and he cared for the church organization. He told them what he expected of them, but she wrote, "I don't think he really expects anything of us."

Abraham Lincoln went to church one Sunday with a friend. Later, at the noon meal, the friend asked, "What did you think of the preacher?" Lincoln replied, "He was tall and a good speaker."

"But you didn't answer my question," the friend said.

"Did you like the preacher?"

"No," Lincoln replied.

"Why?" asked the friend.

"Because he did not ask us to do anything for God."

The aim of the sermon should be to move listeners to take some type of action—an action that they would not have taken without the sermon. The sermon is supposed to make a difference in someone's life. Every person should leave as a different person.

7. Effective preaching is truth given through personality.

Preaching is more than a well-written manuscript—even one filled with important truths. It is the sum of the sermon material and all the communicating skills one can bring to the occasion.

Communication experts today tell us that the words we speak count for only about 7 percent of what is communicated. Thirty-eight percent comes from the voice—tonal expressions, rhythms, and fluctuations. A whopping 55 percent is nonverbal—gestures, facial expressions, our stance, and eye contact. These figures indicate the need for each of us to reevaluate our preaching.

As a bishop, I read many sermons by pastors who were having trouble preaching, or having problems with their congregations related to their preaching.

For the most part, the sermon material was adequate. It became apparent that it was not the content that was lacking, but the presentation. These preachers are similar to musicians who could play the notes but not the music. Good preaching involves the whole person. It involves more—much more than just the mind. When you stand in a pulpit to preach, you are a person—not an machine playing a recording.

What a shame to have good news and not be able to proclaim it!

These are seven hallmarks of effective preaching. Study them and apply them to your own proclamation.

The Final Preparation

Absorbing and Being Absorbed
by the Sermon

The time between writing and the actual delivery
of the sermon is critical. The manuscript is ready, but is
the preacher?

This is the ripening time for both the preacher and the
sermon. All of us know that bananas need time to ripen,
so do sermons.

The ripening time for the preacher and the sermon is
complicated by the Sunday morning deadline. Sunday
comes so often. How many times have I heard Jesus'
words, "My time has not yet come" (John 7:6). Of course,
Jesus was not talking about a sermon, but his words about
himself have reflected my feelings about preaching a sermon that needed a little more time to ripen.

The preparation for preaching does not end with the
written sermon. From the time the sermon idea is planted
like a seed in your mind, God has been present offering
guidance, direction, insight, and wisdom.

When you are preparing to actually preach, you need
God's help even more. Representing God as a herald of his

Word, standing in a dedicated pulpit demands a special spiritual underpinning.

A pastor once told me about his new prayer life. He said, "I do not know whether God has done anything for the people I have prayed for, but over the months, God has really worked me over." We need God to work us over as we prepare to preach. We need God to be so much a part of us that we can be transformed into people of power.

From the scripture, we learn that when Jesus dwelt in the presence of God, his countenance was altered. Not only was his soul filled, but also his expression changed. Every change took place when he was with God in prayer. The renewing work of God in us can even show in our faces as well as in our words.

The prayer of St. Francis begins with the cry, "Lord, make me an instrument . . ." If only we could become God's instruments in his pulpits. No preacher in his or her right mind should enter the pulpit without recognizing that sermons must be delivered by the preacher and by God.

Regardless of how much time you spent writing your sermon, now you must get the sermon into your mind. All pastors do not use the same method of delivery. Some preach from a manuscript, others from notes, and still others without either. All methods require mental preparation.

The degree of preparation necessary is determined by the preaching skills of the preacher, the content of the sermon, and the amount of time spent in writing the sermon.

Some people seem to have photographic memories. They can finish their writing and deliver sermons almost verbatim. Others are not as fortunate. For everyone, however, the sermon must find a secure lodging place in the mind.

THE FINAL PREPARATION

Before you preach, allow plenty of time to digest your sermon. Live with it on two or three different occasions. Read and reread your sermon, silently and aloud. I do so eight or ten times until I capture the essence of the message. Then quietly reflect upon each part, sometimes starting with the introduction and at other times, thinking about it in sections. The night before you preach, spend two or three hours reflecting on your sermon. I find if I do so, then while I sleep, the sermon plays in my mind. This mental "filling" is crucial to good preaching.

The final wrap-up of the preparation period is on Sunday morning. Quiet reflection with both God and my sermon helps me get ready to go into the pulpit.

E P I L O G U E

One day I was standing outside the chancel waiting to enter for a funeral service. An anxious, concerned acolyte standing nearby knew what he was supposed to do, even though it was his first funeral, but he was unsure about the rest of us.

He asked, "What are you going to do in there?" I explained the order of the service and told him I was going to talk about death.

With a serious look, the acolyte asked, "Can you do anything to heal the hurt of the family in there?"

The Sunday morning service does not center on the experience of death, but there are hurting people in every congregation. Perhaps unknowingly, many are seeking something that will give them meaning and purpose in life.

As the young acolyte asked, when you go into the pulpit, "Can you do something to bring healing, hope, and peace to those inside?" This is no unimportant matter.

The sermon to be preached may have been in progress for a month or even a year. A seed was planted, carefully nurtured, and hours of prayer and research have brought fruition to the message.

The sermon's worth is now in the balance. God has called you to proclaim the Word. You have been chosen. What a blessing! What a privilege!

NOTES

Chapter 2. Roadblocks to Faithfulness

1. Phil Barnhart, *More Seasonings for Sermons* (Lima: CSS of Ohio, 1985), 114.

Chapter 4. Unlocking the Workshop

1. John R. Stott, *Between Two Worlds: The Art of Preaching in the Twentieth Century* (Grand Rapids: Wm. B. Eerdmans, 1982), 211-12.
2. *The Executive Speechwriter's Newsletter*, vol. 9, 1 (1994):7.

Chapter 7. Preparing to Build a Sermon

1. John R. Stott, *Between Two Worlds: The Art of Preaching in the Twentieth Century* (Grand Rapids: Wm. B. Eerdmans, 1982), 211-212.
2. Ibid., 220.

Chapter 8. Starting Construction

1. John R. Stott, *Between Two Worlds: The Art of Preaching in the Twentieth Century* (Grand Rapids: Wm. B. Eerdmans, 1982), 211-212.
2. Ibid., 213.

BIBLIOGRAPHY

Barnhart, Phil. *More Seasonings for Sermons.* Lima: CSS of Ohio, 1985.

Barth, Karl. *Church Dogmatics: A Selection.* Magnolia, MA: Peter Smith Publishers, n.d.

Bartlett's Familiar Quotations, Fifteenth Edition. Boston: Little, Brown, and Company, 1968.

Brother Lawrence. *The Practice of the Presence of God.* Translated by Donald Attwater. Springfield, IL: Templegate, 1981.

Cueni, Robert. *The Vital Church Leader.* Effective Church Series, edited by Herb L. Miller. Nashville: Abingdon Press, 1991.

The Executive Speechwriter's Newsletter (St. Johnsbury, VT) 9, no. 1 (1994):7.

Hickman, Hoyt, ed. *Seasons of the Gospel.* Nashville: Abingdon Press, 1979.

Merton, Thomas. *Seven Storey Mountain.* San Diego: Harcourt Brace & Co., 1978.

Shawchuck, Norman, and Roger Heuser. *Leading the Congregation.* Nashville: Abingdon Press, 1993.

Stott, John R. *Between Two Worlds: The Art of Preaching in the Twentieth Century.* Grand Rapids: Wm. B. Eerdmans, 1982.

Trueblood, Elton, *While It Is Day.* Richmond: Yokefellow Press, 1983.

The United Methodist Book of Worship. Nashville: The United Methodist Publishing House, 1992.